The World of the Ancient Greeks

STEP BACK IN TIME 3,000 YEARS to the shores of the eastern Mediterranean where one of the most enduring and influential civilizations of the Western world is emerging. Ancient Greece was made up of a number of self-supporting city states, each of which developed a strong, individual identity. They developed from an agricultural society that wrote in simple pictograms into a sophisticated culture. Centuries on, the Greek legacy survives in parts of modern society. The origins of democracy, mathematics, medicine and philosophy can be traced back to this time in history. Even some of our words are made up from ancient Greek. "Telephone" comes from the ancient Greek words "tele" meaning far and "phonos" meaning sound.

A FEAT OF PERFECTION
The Parthenon is regarded as the supreme achievement of Greek architecture. It was the most important building in Athens, where it still sits on top of the Acropolis. The temple took 15 years to build and was dedicated to Athena, guardian goddess of Athens. Around 22,000 tonnes of marble, transported from over 15 km away, were used in its construction.

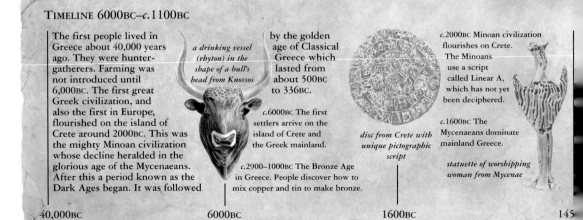

TIMELINE 6000BC–*c.*1100BC

The first people lived in Greece about 40,000 years ago. They were hunter-gatherers. Farming was not introduced until 6,000BC. The first great Greek civilization, and also the first in Europe, flourished on the island of Crete around 2000BC. This was the mighty Minoan civilization whose decline heralded in the glorious age of the Mycenaeans. After this a period known as the Dark Ages began. It was followed by the golden age of Classical Greece which lasted from about 500BC to 336BC.

a drinking vessel (rhyton) in the shape of a bull's head from Knossos

*c.*6000BC The first settlers arrive on the island of Crete and the Greek mainland.

*c.*2900–1000BC The Bronze Age in Greece. People discover how to mix copper and tin to make bronze.

disc from Crete with unique pictographic script

*c.*2000BC Minoan civilization flourishes on Crete. The Minoans use a script called Linear A, which has not yet been deciphered.

*c.*1600BC The Mycenaeans dominate mainland Greece.

statuette of worshipping woman from Mycenae

40,000BC   6000BC   1600BC   145

THE ANCIENT GREEK WORLD

The map above shows the main ports and cities through which the Greeks traded. The ancient Greek world centred on the Aegean Sea. The Greeks were adventurous seafarers. Trade took them from the Aegean Sea to the Atlantic Ocean and the shores of the Black Sea, where they formed many settlements. These colonies helped Greece to spread its influence beyond the mainland and its offshore islands.

CENTRE STONE

The omphalos (navel) was a carved stone kept at the shrine at Delphi. The ancient Greeks thought that this holy sanctuary was the centre of the world. The omphalos stone was placed there to mark the centre. It was said to have been put there by Zeus, ruler of the gods. It may have also served as an altar on which sacrifices were made.

THE PAST REVEALED

Archaeological evidence in the shape of pottery such as this vase help us to piece together the history of Greece. This vase is typical of the superior craftsmanship for which the Greeks were admired. It was common for vases to be decorated with pictures showing historical events. In this one, we see a scene from the siege of Troy in which the king is being murdered. The siege was an important event in Greek folklore. These decorative vases were used as containers for liquids such as oil, water and wine. The export of such pottery contributed an enormous amount of wealth to the Greek empire.

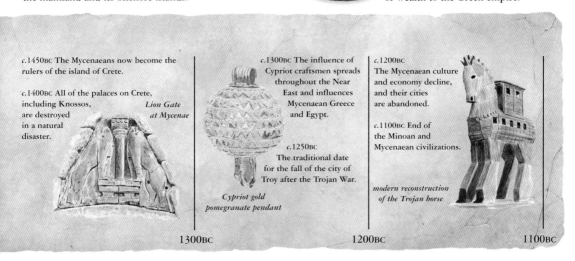

*c.*1450BC The Mycenaeans now become the rulers of the island of Crete.

*c.*1400BC All of the palaces on Crete, including Knossos, are destroyed in a natural disaster.

Lion Gate at Mycenae

*c.*1300BC The influence of Cypriot craftsmen spreads throughout the Near East and influences Mycenaean Greece and Egypt.

*c.*1250BC
The traditional date for the fall of the city of Troy after the Trojan War.

Cypriot gold pomegranate pendant

*c.*1200BC
The Mycenaean culture and economy decline, and their cities are abandoned.

*c.*1100BC End of the Minoan and Mycenaean civilizations.

modern reconstruction of the Trojan horse

1300BC   1200BC   1100BC

Power and Prosperity

THE HISTORY OF ANCIENT GREECE spans 20 centuries. It starts with the Minoan civilization on the island of Crete, which reached its height between 1900 and 1450BC. This culture was also the first to develop in Europe. The Minoans were a lively and artistic people who built palaces and towns and were also great seafarers. Their achievements greatly influenced the Mycenaeans, who built their own civilization on the Greek mainland from around 1600BC. Both the Minoan and Mycenaean cultures collapsed, probably under the impact of natural disasters and warfare, to be followed by centuries of poverty.

Revival was under way by 750BC and the Greek world reached its economic peak during the 5th century BC. This period is known as the Classical Age, when Athens was at the height of its power and prosperity. During this century, Athens led the Greeks into many victorious battles against Persia. However, Athens itself later suffered an economic decline because of a series of wars fought against its rival, Sparta. Then, in the 4th century BC, Greece was conquered by Macedonia. The Macedonian ruler Alexander the Great spread Greek culture throughout his empire. Finally, between 168 and 146BC Macedonia and Greece were absorbed into the Roman empire, and Greek civilization became part of the heritage that Rome passed on to the rest of Europe.

TRADE AND EXPANSION
The Classical Age in Greek history dates from around 500 to 336BC. This period was marked by an increase in the wealth of most Greek city states. Greek trade ships were sailing throughout the Mediterranean and Black Sea. Colonies were also being set up on the shorelines of these two seas.

ITALY

• *Locri*

SICILY
• *Naxos*

• *Syracuse*

N

W   E

S

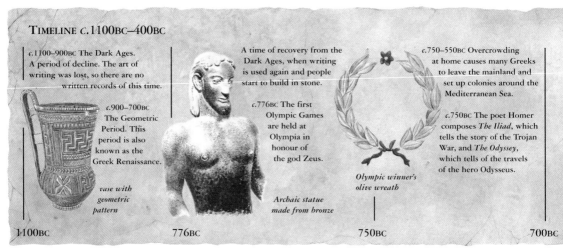

TIMELINE c.1100BC–400BC

c.1100–900BC The Dark Ages. A period of decline. The art of writing was lost, so there are no written records of this time.

c.900–700BC The Geometric Period. This period is also known as the Greek Renaissance.

vase with geometric pattern

A time of recovery from the Dark Ages, when writing is used again and people start to build in stone.

c.776BC The first Olympic Games are held at Olympia in honour of the god Zeus.

Archaic statue made from bronze

Olympic winner's olive wreath

c.750–550BC Overcrowding at home causes many Greeks to leave the mainland and set up colonies around the Mediterranean Sea.

c.750BC The poet Homer composes *The Iliad*, which tells the story of the Trojan War, and *The Odyssey*, which tells of the travels of the hero Odysseus.

1100BC   776BC   750BC   700BC

STEP INTO...

ANCIENT GREECE

Richard Tames

Consultant: Louise Schofield

HERMES
HOUSE

This edition is published by Hermes House

Hermes House is an imprint of
Anness Publishing Ltd
Hermes House, 88–89 Blackfriars Rd,
London SE1 8HA
tel. 020 7401 2077; fax 020 7633 9499;
info@anness.com

Publisher: Joanna Lorenz
Managing Editor, Children's Books: Sue Grabham
Project Editor: Joanne Hanks
Editor: Linda Sonntag
Editorial Reader: Joy Wotton
Designer: Stuart Watkinson at Ideas Into Print
Illustration: Robert Ashby, Stuart Carter, Shane Marsh
Photography: John Freeman
Stylist: Thomasina Smith
Additional Styling: Melanie Williams
Production Controller: Ann Childers

Anness Publishing would like to thank the following children
for modelling for this book: Lucilla Braune, Aileen Greiner,
Francesca Hill, Daniel Ofori, Vanessa Ofori, Edward Parker,
Claudia Martins Silva, Cleon Smith, Nicky Stafford, Saif
Uddowlla, Kirsty Wells. Gratitude also to their parents, and to
Hampden Gurney and Walnut Tree Walk Schools.

PICTURE CREDITS
b=bottom, t=top, c=centre, l=left, r=right
Ancient Art and Architecture Collection Ltd: pages 5tr, 8cr, 9br,
11cl, 12cr, 15tl, 18tl, 21br, 21bl, 22tl, 22cl, 24cr, 25br, 27tr, 27cl,
30tr, 32tl, 32cl, 33c, 35cr, 38bl, 39tr, 40cr, 41cl, 42tl, 46tr, 48cl,
49tr, 51br, 54cl, 56bl, 57cl, 58tr, 60tl; Bildarchiv Preussischer
Kulturbesitz: page 38tl; Bridgeman Art Library: pages 5cr, 16bl,
20br, 29t, 32tr, 34cl, 34tr, 43r; British Museum: pages 12tl, 12bl,
31cl, 35cl, 41tl; Peter Clayton: pages 15bl, 19br, 24tl, 30cl, 31tr,
39b, 53tr, 55tl, 55cl; C M Dixon: pages 4c, 8c, 9tr, 9cl, 10c, 11tl,
11cr, 13c, 16tr, 16br, 17tr, 17cl, 17br, 19cl, 19bl, 20cl, 23tr, 24bl,
25tl, 26cl, 27tl, 27cr, 28tr, 28c, 29cl, 33tr, 36tl, 39tl, 39cl, 40tl,
41tr, 45tl, 47cl, 52tr, 52cl, 56tr, 56br, 57bl, 58cl, 59tr, 61br; Mary
Evans Picture Library: pages 8tl, 9tl, 10tl, 13b, 14tr, 34c, 43bl,
45tr, 50tr, 53cl, 54tl, 54cr, 56cl, 59cl, 60bl, 61tr, 61cl; Sonia
Halliday Photographs: pages 20tl, 21tr; Robert Harding Associates:
pages 13t, 60br; Michael Holford: pages 19tr, 26cr, 30tl, 31tl, 35tr,
36cr, 43tl, 45cl, 46cl, 47tr, 50bl, 51cr, 57tr; Michael Nicholson:
pages 11tr, 14c, 15tr, 18bl, 37tl, 37cl, 37bl, 44tr, 44cl, 51tl, 51cl,
51bl.

Printed and bound in China

10 9 8 7 6 5 4 3 2 1

CONTENTS

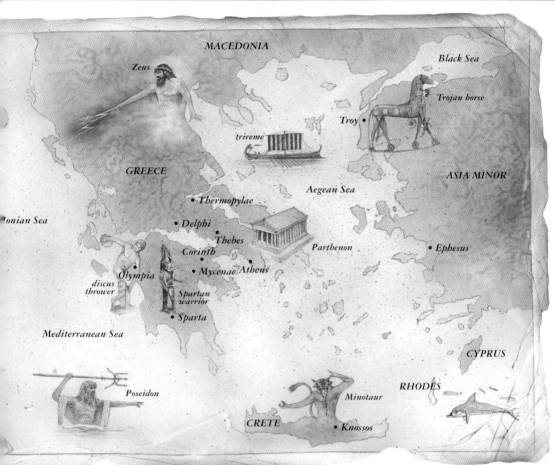

MACEDONIA

Zeus

Black Sea

Trojan horse

Troy •

trireme

GREECE

ASIA MINOR

Aegean Sea

• *Thermopylae*

• *Delphi*

onian Sea

Thebes

Corinth

Parthenon

• *Ephesus*

• *Mycenae* Athens

Olympia

discus thrower

Spartan warrior

• *Sparta*

Mediterranean Sea

CYPRUS

Poseidon

RHODES

Minotaur

CRETE

• *Knossos*

---

*c.*700–500BC The Archaic Period. During this period Greece expands. Athens becomes the largest and most influential of the independent city states that make up Greece.

*c.*508BC Democracy is introduced in Athens. Every citizen has the right to speak and vote.

Odysseus gouges out the eye of a Cyclops

*c.*500–336BC The Classical Age. Greek culture and learning reaches its height.

*c.*480–479BC The Persian Wars. The Greeks are victorious, defeating the Persians at the battles of Marathon and Salamis.

Persian archer

*c.*479–431BC The golden age of Athens. Trade flourishes and the city grows very prosperous.

*c.*447–432BC The Parthenon is built in Athens.

the Parthenon

500BC   479BC   443BC

Famous Greeks

THE GREEKS TREASURED THEIR rich store of myths and legends about gods and heroes, but they also took a keen interest in human history. They valued fame and glory far more than riches. Their ultimate aim in life was to make a name for themselves that would live on long after death. Statues were put up in prominent places to honour Greeks who had won fame in different ways – as generals on the battlefield, as poets, teachers, philosophers, mathematicians, orators or sportsmen. These heroes represented the human qualities the Greeks most admired – physical courage, endurance and strength, and the intelligence to create, invent, explain and persuade.

HOMER (c700BC)

The blind poet Homer (above) was honoured for writing two epic tales. The first is *The Iliad,* a story about the siege of Troy. The other is *The Odyssey* which follows the adventures of Odysseus in his travels after the battle of Troy. Scholars now believe that the tales may have been written by two poets or even groups of several poets.

SAPPHO (c600BC)

The poet Sappho was born on the island of Lesbos. She wrote nine books of poetry, but only one complete poem survives. Beauty and love were the subjects of her poetry. Her work inspired other artists of the time and influenced many writers and poets in later centuries.

SOPHOCLES (496–406BC)

Only seven of Sophocles' plays have survived. He is thought to have written 123 altogether. Besides being a playwright, Sophocles was also a respected general and politician. His name means "famed for wisdom".

TIMELINE 440BC–140BC

443–429BC The great statesman, Pericles, dominates politics in Athens.

431–404BC The Peloponnesian Wars take place between Athens and its great rival, Sparta. The Spartans defeat the Athenians.

399BC The Athenian philosopher, Socrates is condemned to death because his views prove unpopular.

marble bust of the philosopher, Socrates

371BC Sparta is defeated by Thebes. Thebes becomes the leading power in Greece.

362BC Sparta and Athens combine forces to defeat the Thebans at the battle of Mantinea.

338BC The Greeks are defeated by the Macedonians at the battle of Chaeronea. Philip II of Macedonia becomes ruler of Greece.

iron corselet which is thought to have belonged to Philip II of Macedonia

336BC Philip II of Macedonia dies and is succeeded by his son, Alexander the Great. Alexander builds a huge empire, stretching from Greece as far east as India.

bronze statuette of Alexander the Great

443BC   371BC   336BC   334BC

PERICLES (495–429BC)

A popular figure and brilliant public speaker, Pericles was elected as a general 20 times. While in office, he built up a powerful navy and organized the building of strong defences, beautiful temples and fine monuments. He also gave ordinary citizens more say in government. Pericles' career ended after he led Athens into a disastrous war against Sparta. He was ostracized (expelled) as punishment for his misjudgement.

ALEXANDER THE GREAT (356–323BC)

Alexander was the son of Philip II of Macedonia. His life was spent in conquest of new territory, and his empire stretched across the Middle East, Persia and Afghanistan as far as the river Indus. His empire was swiftly divided when he died after suspected poisoning.

SOCRATES (469–399BC)

A renowned teacher and philosopher, Socrates encouraged people to think about how to live a good life. The Athenians sentenced him to die by drinking hemlock (a poison). Plato, Socrates' most brilliant pupil and himself a great philosopher, recorded his teacher's last days.

ARCHIMEDES (287–211BC)

The mathematician, scientist, astronomer and inventor, Archimedes came from Syracuse. When his city was besieged by the Romans, he designed a huge lens that focused sunlight on the Roman ships and set them on fire. He also devised a screw for raising water out of the ground and studied the concepts of floating and balance.

334BC Alexander the Great invades Persia to include it in his empire.

333BC The Persian army, led by King Darius, is defeated by Alexander the Great at the battle of Issus.

331BC Alexander the Great becomes king of Persia after defeating the Persians at the battle of Gaugamela.

King Darius of Persia

Romulus and Remus, legendary founders of Rome

323BC Alexander the Great dies, and his successors fight over the throne.

275BC Greek colonies are taken over by the Romans.

168BC Rome defeats the Macedonian rulers of Greece.

147–146BC The Achaean War. The Romans take control of Greece and Macedonia.

Roman soldier in full armour

323BC   196BC   146BC

9

The Minoans

AT THE HEART OF THE MINOAN CIVILIZATION was a huge palace at Knossos. The palace was a great political and cultural centre, and it controlled much of central Crete. At the height of its prosperity around 2000BC, over 10,000 people lived in the palace. Despite its obvious wealth, the palace was left unfortified because its rulers believed that their fleet could overcome any invaders. However, around 1450BC, the warlike Mycenaean Greeks captured Knossos and destroyed all the other Minoan palaces and towns.

In the early 1900s, British archaeologist Sir Arthur Evans unearthed the splendid remains of an ancient civilization on the island of Crete. He named it "Minoan" after the legendary Cretan king Minos, son of Zeus. It was discovered that the Minoans did not speak Greek and their writing, known as Linear A, has still not been decoded.

PURPOSEFUL POT
This brightly decorated pot from Knossos was probably used to hold water or wine. Sir Arthur Evans used the changes in pottery style to work out a chronology of the Minoan civilization. This pot was made around 1700–1550BC, on a potter's wheel.

A SPECIAL OCCASION
Frescoes were a popular art form used to decorate the walls of Cretan palaces. In order to make them last, frescoes were painted straight on to the wet plaster walls. This fresco shows a group of women gathered to watch a show or ceremony. Brightly coloured outfits with tight bodices and flounced skirts, as worn by the women here, were typical of the period.

MINOAN SEAL
You will need: work board, white and brown self-drying modelling clay, rolling pin, modelling tool, ruler, needle, PVA glue, water, mixing bowl, paintbrush, soft cord.

1 Roll out a small piece of white self drying modelling clay until it is about 1cm thick. Using a modelling tool, cut a small circle 3cm in diameter.

2 With the modelling tool carve the pattern shown above into the white clay. Leave to dry. This piece is the mould for the seal.

3 Roll a piece of the brown clay into a circle 2cm thick, and 3·5cm in diameter. Gently press the mould into the clay to leave an imprint.

Pillars were used to support the upper floors within the palace. They were made from wood, and painted in bright colours.

LIVING IN LUXURY

The queen had her own set of apartments in the magnificent palace at Knossos. A large fresco decorates the wall in this room. It shows lively dolphins and fish swimming underwater. Most Minoan frescoes show scenes from palace life and the natural world. The paintings are a vital source of information for modern historians.

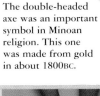

PALACE COMPLEX

The ruins of the great palace complex at Knossos have been excavated and partially reconstructed. Many of the Cretan palaces seem to have expanded with the random addition of rooms and corridors. Knossos was the largest of these palaces.

ROYAL SYMBOL

The double-headed axe was an important symbol in Minoan religion. This one was made from gold in about 1800BC.

A DANGEROUS DANCE

Bull-leaping was a popular form of entertainment in Crete. Both men and women took part in the sport. The young person would somersault over a charging bull's horns and then leap off its back. This sport may have been part of a religious rite.

4 Cut around the imprint leaving an edge 1cm wide. Make 2 small holes on each side of the circle with the needle. Leave to dry. This piece is the seal.

5 Prepare the varnish by mixing 2 parts of glue to 1 part of water. Brush the seal with varnish. Make sure that the holes aren't filled in with it.

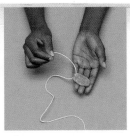

6 Leave the varnish to dry. Cut a length of cord and thread it through either one or both holes. Wear it on your wrist or around your neck.

Seals were used as an identity badge, as a sign of ownership, as a lucky charm or as a piece of art.

The Mycenaeans

The first important civilization on mainland Greece developed in the north-eastern part of the Peloponnese between 1600 and 1200BC. A series of small kingdoms and great fortresses were built during this period. The most powerful of these kingdoms was Mycenae. The Mycenaeans did not keep historical records, and therefore our knowledge of them comes largely from archaelogical evidence. We know that they were an advanced culture as they communicated in a written language and developed technology.

The Mycenaeans had the ability to quarry and build. Excavations have revealed high walls made from huge stone slabs. They learnt how to sail ships and developed extensive trade routes to Egypt, the Near East and the Baltic Sea. From these distant shores they imported gold, tin to make bronze, and amber for jewellery. Local resources such as olive trees were exploited for large financial gain.

Oil was extracted from the olives, then perfumed and bottled for export.

Around 1200BC the Mycenaean culture suffered an economic recession that led to its downfall. Historians believe that earthquakes, wars and fires may have triggered the recession.

FRUIT OF LABOUR
This gold pomegranate pendant was found in a tomb on the island of Cyprus. The surface is decorated with fine grains of gold using a process known as the granulation technique. It took a skilled artist to make such a detailed piece of jewellery.

BOAR HELMET
The Mycenaeans favoured elaborate armour, such as this 13th-century BC helmet plated with boar's tusks. Other materials used to make armour included linen, leather and bronze. A great deal of weaponry has been excavated from the royal shaft graves at Mycenae.

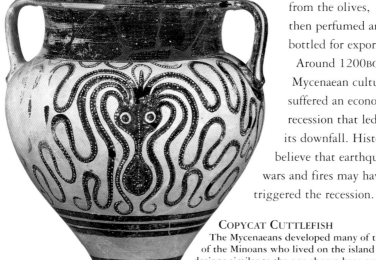

COPYCAT CUTTLEFISH
The Mycenaeans developed many of their ideas from those of the Minoans who lived on the island of Crete. Cuttlefish designs similar to the one shown here are also found on Minoan pottery. Mycenaean pottery was widely traded and has been found as far away as northern Italy and eastern Spain. Small jars for holding perfumed olive oil were among the most popular wares.

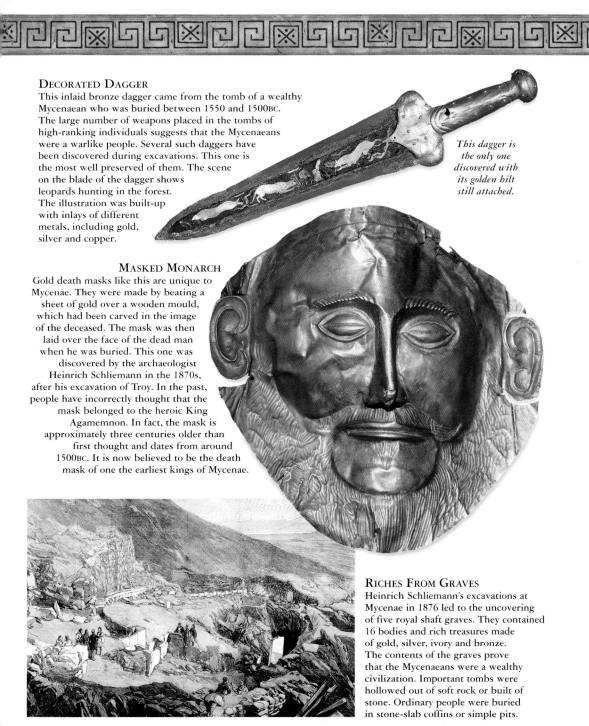

DECORATED DAGGER

This inlaid bronze dagger came from the tomb of a wealthy
Mycenaean who was buried between 1550 and 1500BC.
The large number of weapons placed in the tombs of
high-ranking individuals suggests that the Mycenaeans
were a warlike people. Several such daggers have
been discovered during excavations. This one is
the most well preserved of them. The scene
on the blade of the dagger shows
leopards hunting in the forest.
The illustration was built-up
with inlays of different
metals, including gold,
silver and copper.

*This dagger is
the only one
discovered with
its golden hilt
still attached.*

MASKED MONARCH

Gold death masks like this are unique to
Mycenae. They were made by beating a
sheet of gold over a wooden mould,
which had been carved in the image
of the deceased. The mask was then
laid over the face of the dead man
when he was buried. This one was
discovered by the archaeologist
Heinrich Schliemann in the 1870s,
after his excavation of Troy. In the past,
people have incorrectly thought that the
mask belonged to the heroic King
Agamemnon. In fact, the mask is
approximately three centuries older than
first thought and dates from around
1500BC. It is now believed to be the death
mask of one the earliest kings of Mycenae.

RICHES FROM GRAVES

Heinrich Schliemann's excavations at
Mycenae in 1876 led to the uncovering
of five royal shaft graves. They contained
16 bodies and rich treasures made
of gold, silver, ivory and bronze.
The contents of the graves prove
that the Mycenaeans were a wealthy
civilization. Important tombs were
hollowed out of soft rock or built of
stone. Ordinary people were buried
in stone-slab coffins or simple pits.

Politics and Government

THE GREEK WORLD WAS MADE UP of about 300 separate city states. Some were no bigger than villages, while others centred around cities such as Sparta or Athens. Each city state was known as a *polis* (from which we take our word politics) and had its own laws and government. In the 4th century BC, the Greek philosopher, Aristotle, wrote that there were three types of government. The first was power held by one person. They could either be a king (who ruled on account of his royal birth), or a tyrant (who ruled by force). The second type was government by the few which meant rule by an aristocracy (governing by right of noble birth) or an oligarchy (a ruling group of rich and powerful men). The third type was a democratic government (rule by the many) which gave every male citizen the right to vote, hold public office or serve on a jury. Democracy was only practised in Athens. Even there women, slaves and foreigners were not counted as full citizens.

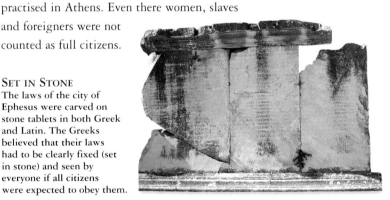

SET IN STONE
The laws of the city of Ephesus were carved on stone tablets in both Greek and Latin. The Greeks believed that their laws had to be clearly fixed (set in stone) and seen by everyone if all citizens were expected to obey them.

BEHIND THE SCENES
Women were not allowed to take an active part in politics in ancient Greece. However, some played an important role behind the scenes. One such woman was Aspasia. As a professional entertainer, she met and became mistress to Pericles (one of the most influential Athenian statesmen of the 5th century BC). Pericles confided in his mistress about affairs of state, and he came to rely on her insight and wisdom in his judgement of people and situations.

VOTING TOKENS
You will need: pair of compasses, thin card, pencil, ruler, scissors, rolling pin, cutting board, self-hardening clay, modelling tool, balsa wood stick 5cm long, piece of drinking straw 5cm long, bronze-coloured paint, paintbrush, water pot.

1 Make two templates. Use a pair of compasses to draw two circles, on a piece of thin card. Make each one 4cm in diameter. Cut them out.

2 Use a rolling pin to roll out the clay to 3cm thickness. Use a modelling tool to cut around the card circles into the clay. Press down hard as you do this.

3 Make a hole in the centre of each clay circle. Use the balsa wood to make one hole (innocent token). Use the straw to make the other hole (guilty token).

PEOPLE POWER

Solon the Lawgiver was an Athenian statesman and poet who lived from 640 to 559BC. Around 594BC, when serving as chief magistrate, he gave Athens new laws that enabled more people to take part in politics. His actions prevented a potential civil war between the few nobles in power and the people who suffered under their rule.

VOTE HERE

This terracotta urn was used to collect voting tokens. They were used in Athens when votes needed to be taken in law courts or when the voters' intentions needed to be kept secret. Each voter put a bronze disc in the urn to register his decision. Normally, voting was done by a show of hands, which was difficult to count precisely.

FACE TO FACE

The ruins of this council chamber at Priene in present-day Turkey show how seating was arranged. The tiered, three-sided square enabled each councillor to see and hear clearly all of the speakers involved in a debate. Even in the democracies of ancient Greece, most everyday decisions were taken by committees or councils and not by the assembly of voters.

4 Write a name on the innocent token using the modelling tool. Carefully push the balsa stick through the hole. Leave it to dry.

5 Write another name on the guilty token using the modelling tool. Carefully push the drinking straw through the hole. Leave it to dry.

6 Wait until the clay tokens are dry before painting them. The original tokens were made from bronze, so use a bronze-coloured paint.

Jurors were issued with two tokens to vote with. A hollow centre meant that the juror thought the accused was guilty. A solid centre meant that the juror thought the accused was innocent.

Equality and Inequality

GREEK SOCIETY WAS DIVIDED by a strict social structure, enforced by its governments. Most city states were ruled by a small group of people (*oligarchy*). Two exceptions to this rule were the powerful cities of Sparta and Athens. Sparta held on to its monarchy, while Athens introduced the first democratic government in history. In the city of Athens, all citizens could vote and hold office. However to be a citizen, it was necessary to be an adult male, born in the city itself. Even so-called democratic Athens was ruled by a minority of the people who lived there. The treatment of women, foreign residents (called *metics*), slaves and children was just the same as in other city states.

Women had no legal rights and rarely took part in public life. Metics were obliged to pay extra taxes and serve in the military. They could not own land or marry an Athenian. The Athenians felt uneasy about the large number of metics living in their city, but their skills helped to make it rich. Slaves made up half the population of Athens. Most had either been born slaves or become slaves as prisoners of war or captives of pirates. Even native Greeks could become slaves by falling into debt, but they were freed once the debt was paid off.

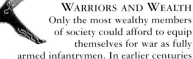

WARRIORS AND WEALTH

Only the most wealthy members of society could afford to equip themselves for war as fully armed infantrymen. In earlier centuries the poor were given supporting jobs, such as slinger or carrier of supplies. They could not afford expensive bronze weapons. However, as cities grew richer, weapons were manufactured at public expense by slaves, and most male citizens were expected to carry arms.

A WOMAN'S PLACE

Greek women spent their lives at home. On this vase, made about 450BC, a woman ties her sandal before going out. As she has attendants, she must be wealthy. Poor women would leave the house to fetch water, work in the fields or shop in the market. Women with slaves, like this one, might leave the home to visit relatives or to pray at a shrine or temple.

LOVED ONES

A young girl and her pet dog are seen on this tombstone from the 4th century BC. The likely expense of such a detailed carving suggests that she was dearly loved. Not all children were cherished. Girl babies, and sick babies of either sex, were often left outside to die. Some were underfed and fell victim to diseases. Greek law required children to support their parents in old age, so childless couples were always keen to adopt and were known to rescue abandoned children.

CRAFTSMAN

This smith could be a slave working in a factory owned by a wealthy man. Most craftsmen were slaves, ex-slaves, or foreign residents (*metics*). They were looked down upon by other citizens. If a master owned a talented slave, he might set the slave up to run his own business. In return, the master would receive a share of the profits. This smith might also have been a free, self-employed man, with his own workshop and a slave or two working as his assistants.

PATH TO POWER?

Being able to read and write in ancient Greece was not an automatic key to success. The Greek alphabet could be learned quite easily. Even slaves could become highly educated scribes. However, illiterate men were unlikely to hold high positions, except perhaps in Sparta, where written records were rarely kept. Although women were denied the right to a formal education, they were often able to read and write enough to keep a record of household stores.

ENSLAVED BY LANGUAGE

This Roman bottle is made in the shape of an African slave girl's head. The Greeks also owned slaves. The Greek philosopher Aristotle argued that some people were "naturally" meant to be slaves. His opinion was shared by many of his countrymen. He felt that this applied most obviously to people who did not speak Greek. Slaves were treated with varying degrees of kindness and hostility. Some were worked to death by their owners, but others had good jobs as clerks or bailiffs. A few hundred slaves were owned by the city of Athens and served as policemen, coin-inspectors and clerks of the court.

The Golden Age of Athens

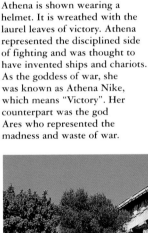

GODDESS OF WAR
On this 4th-century BC coin, Athena is shown wearing a helmet. It is wreathed with the laurel leaves of victory. Athena represented the disciplined side of fighting and was thought to have invented ships and chariots. As the goddess of war, she was known as Athena Nike, which means "Victory". Her counterpart was the god Ares who represented the madness and waste of war.

A THENS WAS THE CHIEF CITY of the fertile region of Attica, in southern Greece. It grew rich from trade, manufacturing and mining silver. The city of Athens reached the height of its wealth and power in the 5th century BC. By this time, it had built up a large empire which encompassed cities on both the mainland and the islands. Its 250,000 citizens enjoyed a vibrant golden age of art and culture. During this period, the Athenians celebrated a victory against Persian invaders by building a series of magnificent temples on the Acropolis in Athens. The Acropolis was a sacred hill that overlooked the city. Its most important temple was the Parthenon, which was dedicated to the city's goddess, Athena. Below, at the heart of the city was the market-place (*agora*). Surrounded by temples and public buildings and crowded with stalls, the agora was the commercial centre of Athens.

Between 431 and 404BC, Athens fought a crippling war against Sparta and the Persians. It lost the war and most of its maritime empire. As a result, Athens gave up its role as commercial and cultural leader in Greece to Sparta.

CROWNING GLORY
This temple to Hephaestus is a supreme example of the elegant architecture at which the Athenians excelled. It was built between 449 and 444BC at the eastern end of the agora. Hephaestus was the god of fire and armourer of the gods. A bronze statue inside the temple showed Hephaestus at work making armour, wearing a blacksmith's cap and holding a hammer above an anvil. Excavations have revealed that the bronze sculptors worked on one side of the temple, while sculptors in marble worked on the other side.

PANATHENAIC FESTIVAL

Every year, the people of Athens marched or rode in a great procession up to Athena's temple on the Acropolis. Even foreign residents joined in. This frieze from the Parthenon shows young men getting ready to join the procession. At the temple, oxen and other animals were sacrificed, and the meat was given to the people to eat. Every fourth year, there was an extra celebration when a new robe (*peplos*) was presented to the goddess Athena. This event was celebrated with days of sporting and musical competitions, with prizes of money or olive oil.

BIRTH OF A GODDESS

According to Greek legend, Zeus swallowed a pregnant lover after a prophecy warned that their child would depose him. Not long after swallowing her, Zeus complained of a painful headache. Hephaestus offered to split open Zeus's head with an axe to ease the pain. When he did, the goddess Athena jumped out. She was fully grown and wearing the armour of a warrior (as seen here in the centre of the painting).

BANISHMENT

Once a year, Athenians were allowed to banish an unpopular member of the community from the city for 10 years. Voters scratched the names on a fragment of pottery called an ostrakon, which is why the procedure was called ostracism. If at least 6,000 votes were cast in favour of exiling a person, they would have to leave the city within 10 days. Ostraka were also used for messages and shopping lists.

GODDESS OF WISDOM

The owl, symbolizing wisdom, was the emblem of Athena. This silver coin was issued in Athens in 479BC, after the Greeks won decisive victories against the Persians. Athenian coins were accepted throughout Greece, Italy and Turkey. This proves just how influential the city of Athens. Coins from other city states were not widely accepted.

The Spartan Order

A T THE HEIGHT OF ITS POWER, Sparta was the only city state to rival the influence of Athens. It controlled most of the area of southern Greece, called the Peloponnese. Sparta was an insular and militaristic state. It became so after losing control of its slave population in a rebellion, which lasted for 17 years. The slaves (helots) were descendants of the people of Messenia whom Sparta overran in the 8th century BC. The helots outnumbered their Spartan overlords by seven to one. Although the Spartans defeated the rebellion, they continued to live in fear of another one. As a result, all male citizens were required by law to serve as full-time warriors. In addition, harsh restrictions were placed on the helots who were forbidden to ride horses or stay out after nightfall. While the citizens were fully occupied with military training, the heavy work and domestic chores were done by the helots.

The Spartans imposed strict living conditions on themselves. Spartan boys and girls were separated from their parents and brought up in barracks. Boys were trained for battle from the age of seven. They were kept cold, barefoot and hungry, and regularly flogged to make them tough. At the age of 20 they joined a group of 15 men who became their comrades. In Sparta, comradeship between men was more important than family life. The girls also took part in physical training so as to be able to bear healthy children. The power of Sparta declined after its defeat by the Theban army in 371 BC.

HEROIC KING
This bust from the 5th century BC may be of King Leonidas. There were two royal familes in Sparta. A king was chosen from each family to govern Sparta at the same time. Their powers were limited. Their main responsibility was to lead Spartan forces into battle.

WINE FOR THE WARRIORS
This massive bronze krater (wine vessel) stands 165 cm high, weighs 208 kg and holds 1,200 l of liquid. It was made around 530 BC by a Spartan craftsman. The neck of the krater is decorated with Spartan warriors and chariots marching to war. The handles are crafted with the heads of female monsters called gorgons. It is thought that the vase was presented as a gift to the king of Lydia who wanted to form an alliance with Sparta. The Spartans were admired for the high quality of their bronze work.

DEATH AND GLORY

This modern monument was erected to commemorate the heroic self-sacrifice of King Leonidas and 300 Spartans. They died in 480BC defending the pass at Thermopylae against a Persian army 250,000 strong. The pass was just 13 m wide and the Spartans held their ground for two days while waiting for reinforcements. On the third day, a traitor showed the invading Persians another way through the mountain. Leonidas ordered a retreat, then led the rearguard in a fight to the death.

SEA POWER

The ivory relief pictured here has a Spartan warship carved into it. The pointed ram at the front was used for sinking enemy ships. Sparta was first and foremost a land power. Its navy was no match for that of Athens. A navy was expensive to run because specialized warships could not be used in peace-time. The Athenians financed their navy from their silver mines, but the Spartans were not so wealthy. They sometimes had to borrow money to keep their navy afloat.

BACKBONE OF THE ARMY

Spartan soldiers were easily distinguished on the battlefield because of their long hair and bright red cloaks. This figurine of a Spartan warrior probably dates from the 6th century BC. His crested helmet incorporates a nose guard and cheek guards. He is also wearing greaves (armour to guard his lower legs) and a cuirass (armour to protect his chest).

LAW-GIVER

This Roman mosaic probably shows the figure of Lycurgus, wielding an axe. Little is known of his life, because so few records were kept in Sparta. It is generally believed that Lycurgus lived around 650BC. His main achievement was to re-organize the government of Sparta for effective warfare after its disastrous defeat by the state of Argos.

At Home

the roof was made of pottery tiles

G REEK HOMES WERE BUILT of mud bricks and roofed with pottery tiles. They had small high windows with wooden shutters to keep out thieves, and floors of beaten earth, plaster or mosaic. Most houses started as small structures, and more rooms were added as the owner could afford them. This gave homes a random appearance and meant that streets were rarely straight. In country areas, houses were often surrounded by a stone wall to protect the inhabitants and their domestic animals. Men and women lived in separate rooms and in different areas of the house. The women's quarters were usually found at the rear of the house. Richer households might also have rooms for cooking and bathing in. Most homes contained only a few pieces of plain furniture which might include couches that doubled as beds, chairs and tables. Only wealthier people could afford richly decorated furniture such as couches inlaid with gold and ivory.

the andron was the room in which men entertained

the mosaic floor was made from brightly coloured pebbles

HOME HEATING
In mountainous areas of Greece, the winter can be very cold. This bronze brazier, dating from the 4th century BC, would have been filled with charcoal and used to heat a chilly room.

HEARTH GODDESS
Hestia was the goddess of the hearth and home. A fire was kept burning in her honour all year round. This fire was used for cooking, for heating water and to make charcoal as fuel for the braziers. Traditionally, when the Greeks founded a colony overseas, they took with them fire from their old home to link the new with the old.

DOLPHIN FRESCO
You will need: pencil, sheet of white paper 21cm x 19cm, rolling pin, white self-hardening clay, ruler, cutting board, modelling tool, pin, sandpaper, paintbrush, acrylic paints, water.

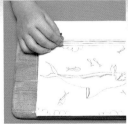

1 Draw a dolphin on the piece of white paper. Add some smaller fish and some seaweed. Refer to the final picture as a guide for your drawing.

2 Roll out a piece of clay until it measures 21cm across and 19cm down. The clay should be about 0.5cm thick. Cut off any uneven edges.

3 While the clay is still damp, place the dolphin picture over it. Following the outline of your picture, prick holes through the paper on to the clay.

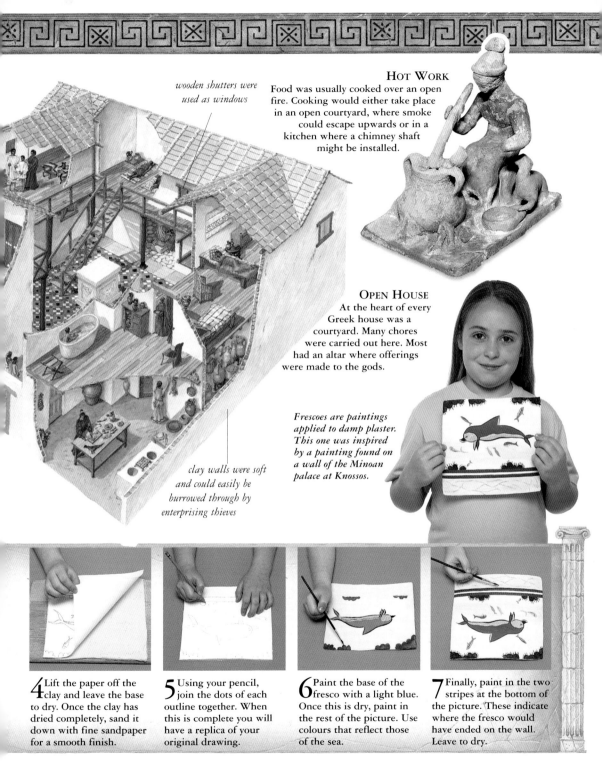

wooden shutters were used as windows

HOT WORK

Food was usually cooked over an open fire. Cooking would either take place in an open courtyard, where smoke could escape upwards or in a kitchen where a chimney shaft might be installed.

OPEN HOUSE

At the heart of every Greek house was a courtyard. Many chores were carried out here. Most had an altar where offerings were made to the gods.

Frescoes are paintings applied to damp plaster. This one was inspired by a painting found on a wall of the Minoan palace at Knossos.

clay walls were soft and could easily be burrowed through by enterprising thieves

4 Lift the paper off the clay and leave the base to dry. Once the clay has dried completely, sand it down with fine sandpaper for a smooth finish.

5 Using your pencil, join the dots of each outline together. When this is complete you will have a replica of your original drawing.

6 Paint the base of the fresco with a light blue. Once this is dry, paint in the rest of the picture. Use colours that reflect those of the sea.

7 Finally, paint in the two stripes at the bottom of the picture. These indicate where the fresco would have ended on the wall. Leave to dry.

Country Living

MOST GREEKS LIVED IN the countryside and worked as farmers. The mountainous landscape, poor, stony soil and hot, dry climate restricted what crops they could produce and which animals they could keep. Olive trees and bees flourished in these conditions. Olives provided oil and bees supplied honey (the main sweetener in food) and wax. Grain, such as barley, was difficult to grow, and the land used for its production had to be left fallow every other year to recover its fertility. Country people kept oxen to pull ploughs and drag heavy loads, and they used donkeys to carry goods to market. Rural areas also produced important materials used by city craftworkers. These included timber, flax for linen, horn and bone for glue, and leather.

Country life was hazardous, as droughts, floods, wolves and warfare threatened their livelihoods. Over the centuries, another problem developed. As forests were cut down for timber and fuel, soil erosion increased, leaving even less fertile land. The search for new agricultural land prompted the growth of Greek colonies along the shores of the Mediterranean and the Black Sea.

OLIVE HARVEST
This vase shows men shaking and beating the branches of an olive tree to bring down its fruit. Olives were eaten and also crushed to extract their oil. The oil was used for cooking, cleaning, as a medicine and a fuel for lamps.

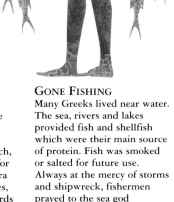

GONE FISHING
Many Greeks lived near water. The sea, rivers and lakes provided fish and shellfish which were their main source of protein. Fish was smoked or salted for future use. Always at the mercy of storms and shipwreck, fishermen prayed to the sea god Poseidon to save them.

FOOD FOR THE POT
Meat was obtained through hunting and the rearing of domesticated animals. Hunting was considered a sport for the rich, but it was a serious business for the poor, who hoped to put extra food on their tables. Simple snares, nets and slings were used to trap lizards and hares and to bring down small birds.

PLOUGHING WITH OXEN

This terracotta figure from Thebes shows a farmer ploughing with two oxen. The plough was made of wood, but the part that broke up the earth was tipped with iron. Oxen were stronger and less expensive than horses, making them ideal for heavy work. When oxen died, they yielded hides for leather as well as horn, meat, sinew, which was used as twine, and fat that could be turned into candle tallow.

SNACKS

Drying food was a good way of preserving it in a warm country like Greece. The Greeks ate raisins and dried apricots as a dessert or used them to sweeten other foods. Olives were another popular snack or appetizer.

olives

apricots

raisins

HARVEST GODDESS

Demeter was the goddess of grain and growth. She looked after plants, children and young people. The first part of her name *deme* is an ancient word for the Earth, the second part, *meter*, means "mother". Farmers believed that their success depended on uncontrollable forces such as the rain, the Sun, and diseases which attacked plants and livestock. Special prayers and sacrifices were made to Demeter to ask for her help in preventing such disasters. Festivals were held in honour of the goddess at crucial times during the harvest, before ploughing, when the corn began to sprout, and after it had been harvested.

25

Food and Drink

MEALS IN ANCIENT GREECE were based around home-baked bread, fish fresh from the sea and such vegetables as onions, beans, lentils, leeks and radishes. Chickens and pigeons were kept for their eggs and meat, and a cow or a few goats or sheep for milk and cheese. Occasionally a pig or goat was slaughtered for the table, or hunting provided boar, deer, hares and even thrushes. The Greeks cooked their meat in olive oil and flavoured it with garlic and wild herbs. They ate fruits such as figs, apples, pears and pomegranates, which could be dried for the winter months. During hard times, people resorted to eating wild berries, hedgehogs and even locusts. Wine was the Greeks' favourite drink. It was usually very thick and had to be strained and then diluted with water for drinking. Sometimes it was mixed with resin, a preservative extracted from pine trees. It could then be kept for three to four years.

WASTE CONVERTER
This terracotta figure shows a butcher killing a pig. Pigs were a cheap source of meat because they could be kept on scrubby pasture and fed on acorns and kitchen scraps. Their skins were tanned to make leather and their hooves melted to make glue.

STORAGE ON A GRAND SCALE
Huge storage jars were used by the Greeks to store food and drink. These come from the palace, at Knossos in Crete. They probably contained olive oil, wine and cereals and were capable of holding hundreds of litres. Handmade from clay, they kept food and drink cool in the hot Mediterranean climate.

PANCAKES WITH HONEY AND SESAME SEEDS
You will need: 100g flour, sieve, mixing bowl, fork, 200ml water, 8 tablespoons clear honey, frying pan, 1 tablespoon sesame seeds, spoon, 1 tablespoon oil, spatula.

1 First make the pancake mix. Sieve the flour into a mixing bowl. Then, using a fork stir the water into the flour. Measure the honey into a small bowl.

2 Spoon the honey into the pancake mixture a bit at a time. Mix it with a fork, making sure that there are no lumps in the pancake mixture.

3 Ask an adult to help you with the next two steps. Heat the frying pan. Sprinkle in the sesame seeds and cook until browned. Set aside.

STAFF OF LIFE

A team of bakers prepare bread for the oven in this terracotta model. In big cities, commercial bakeries produced many different kinds of bread. Ordinary loaves were made of barley or wheat flour, speciality breads were flavoured with mountainside herbs, and delicious pastries came drenched in honey.

PLAY THE GAME

The Greeks drank from large, shallow cups such as this one. This picture shows a man playing a drinking game called *kottabos*. After much drinking, guests would compete to see who was most in control of their faculties by throwing the wine left in the bottom of their cup at a target. In another game, guests tried to make the loudest noise with their cup without spilling its contents.

GOD OF WINE

This Roman stone panel shows a procession of revellers following the Greek god Dionysus to a drinking party. Dionysus was the god of wine and was worshipped with special enthusiasm in vine-growing regions such as Athens, Boeotia and Naxos.

SERVICE

A carved relief shows servants carrying bowls of food. At formal banquets, the guests lay on their sides to eat as this was thought to aid digestion. The Greeks adopted this custom from the peoples of Asia. They often ate and drank until they passed out on their couches, leaving the servants to clear away without waking them.

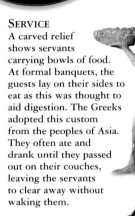

4 Heat a teaspoon of the oil in the frying pan. Pour a quarter of the mix into the pan. Cook on both sides for about 4 minutes, until light brown.

5 Serve the pancake on a plate. Sprinkle on a handful of sesame seeds and pour extra honey over it. Cook the rest of the mix the same way.

Pancakes were a popular snack in ancient Greece, especially with theatre-goers. Food stalls were usually set up around theatres to catch the crowds who had come to view the latest play.

Women at Home

RESPECTABLE GREEK WOMEN were rarely seen out in the public domain. Their lives revolved around the household and family. From an early age, girls were trained in domestic skills which would enable them to run a household once married. A girl might be married off by her father at the age of 13 or 14. Her husband was usually much older and would be given a dowry to offset the costs of providing for her. The purpose of marriage was to produce a son to continue the husband's name. A wife assumed a number of responsibilities in her new home. If she was fortunate to have the help of slaves, she would direct them in their daily tasks. If not, she carried out those chores herself. Chores would include cooking meals, cleaning the house and caring for the children. Some women even managed the family finances.

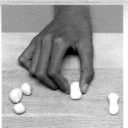

"SO SHE SAID..."
Wealthy women were largely confined to their houses. They often relied on friends or household slaves for news about events in the outside world. Women from poorer families, without slaves, had to leave the house to shop and fetch water. Public fountains were popular meeting places for a gossip.

A CONSTANT TASK
Weaving was considered a respectable occupation for women. This vase painting shows Penelope, wife of the absent hero Odysseus, spinning wool into yarn. Women were expected to produce all the fabric needed to clothe their family. The material they spun was also used for household furnishings such as wall hangings.

KNUCKLEBONES
You will need: self-drying modelling clay, modelling tool, work board, cream paint, paintbrush.

1 Divide the self-drying modelling clay into 5 equal pieces. Roll each piece into a ball. Press each ball into a figure of eight shape, as above.

2 With the modelling tool, carve ridges around the middle of each shape. Make small dents in the end of each shape with your finger.

3 When the pieces have dried out, paint them. Use a cream coloured paint. Once the paint has dried, the pieces are ready to play with.

HOPING FOR HEALTH

Married women from wealthy families rarely left the house. When they did, it was usually to take part in family celebrations or religious ceremonies. The family shown on this carved relief from the 5th century BC are sacrificing a bull to Asclepius, god of health, and Hygieia, his daughter.

Knucklebones were made from the ankle-joints of small animals. These small bones were used in different ways, depending on the type of game. The Greeks also used the knucklebones as dice.

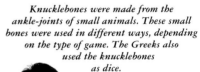

YOUR TURN

Women were supposed to be fully occupied with household tasks. But many kept slaves, which allowed them some leisure time. These women are playing knucklebones. Another favourite pastime was draughts, played on a board with 36 squares.

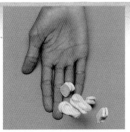

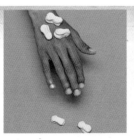

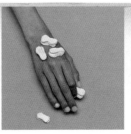

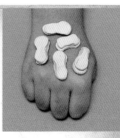

4 To play the game, gather together the five pieces into the palm of one hand. Throw them into the air. Quickly flip your hand over.

5 Try to catch the pieces on the back of your hand. If you're lucky and you catch them all, you win the game. If not, then the game continues.

6 Try to pick up the fallen pieces with the others still on the back of your hand. Throw them with your free hand and try to catch them again.

7 The winner is the first person to have all of the knucklebones on the back of their hand. It may take a few tries for you to get the hang of it.

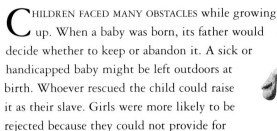

BRINGING UP BABY
This baby is waving a
rattle while sitting in
a high chair. The chair
also served as a potty.
It might have wheels
on it to help the baby
learn how to walk.

Growing Up

CHILDREN FACED MANY OBSTACLES while growing
up. When a baby was born, its father would
decide whether to keep or abandon it. A sick or
handicapped baby might be left outdoors at
birth. Whoever rescued the child could raise
it as their slave. Girls were more likely to be
rejected because they could not provide for
their parents in adulthood. Many children
died in infancy through lack of health-care.

Education was considered to be important for
boys. Even so, it was usually
only sons of rich families who
received a complete schooling.
They were taught a variety
of subjects, including reading,
music and gymnastics. Boys from
poorer families often learnt their
father's trade. Education in
domestic skills was essential for
most girls. A notable exception
was in Sparta, where girls joined
boys in hard physical training.

YOU ARE IT
Two girls play a kind of ta
game in which the loser
has to carry the winner.
Girls had less free time
than boys did. They were
supposed to stay close to
home and help their
mothers with housework,
cooking and looking after
the younger children.

BULLY OFF
These two boys are playing a game similar
to hockey. On the whole, team sports were
ignored in favour of sporting activities
where an individual could excel. Wrestling
and athletics are two such examples. They
were encouraged as training for war.

MAKE A SCROLL
*You will need: 2 x 30cm
rods of balsa wood, 5cm
in diameter, 4 doorknobs,
double-sided sticky tape,
sheet of paper 30cm x 30cm,
1 x 7cm rod of balsa wood,
2cm in diameter, craft
knife, paintbrush, PVA
glue, ink powder.*

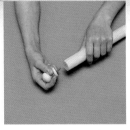

1 Carefully screw a door
knob into either end of
each 30cm rod of balsa
wood, or ask an adult to
do it for you. These are the
end pieces of the scroll.

2 Cut two pieces of
double-sided sticky
tape 30cm long. Stick one
piece of tape along the top
of the paper and another
along the bottom.

3 Wrap the top of the
paper once around one
of the pieces of balsa
wood. Repeat this step
again for the second piece
at the bottom of the paper.

ACTION DOLL

The arms and legs on this terracotta figure are attached with cord so that the shoulders and knees can be moved. A doll such as this was a luxury item, which only a wealthy family could afford to buy for its children. Other popular toys were rattles and hoops.

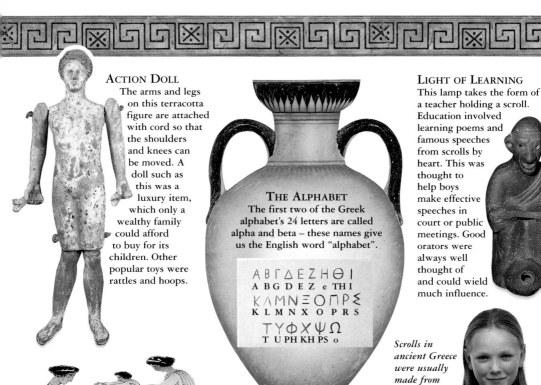

THE ALPHABET

The first two of the Greek alphabet's 24 letters are called alpha and beta – these names give us the English word "alphabet".

ΑΒΓΔΕΖΗΘΙ
A BG DEZ e THI
ΚΛΜΝΞΟΠΡΣ
K LMN X O P R S
ΤΥΦΧΨΩ
T U PH KH PS o

LIGHT OF LEARNING

This lamp takes the form of a teacher holding a scroll. Education involved learning poems and famous speeches from scrolls by heart. This was thought to help boys make effective speeches in court or public meetings. Good orators were always well thought of and could wield much influence.

Scrolls in ancient Greece were usually made from animal skin.

A SECOND MOTHER

Greeks often hired wet nurses (on the left) to breastfeed their babies. Some nurses were forbidden to drink wine in case it affected their milk or made them so drunk that they might harm the baby.

4 Ask an adult to help you with this step. Take the 7cm piece of balsa wood, and use your craft knife to sharpen the end of it into a point.

5 Paint the nib of your pen with glue. This will stop the wood from soaking up the ink. Add water to the ink powder to make ink.

6 Write some letters or a word on your scroll with your pen. We've translated the Greek alphabet above in the fact box. Use this as a guide.

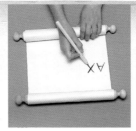

7 We have copied out some letters in ancient Greek. You could also write a word. Ask a friend to translate what you have written, using the alphabet.

Greek Fashion

PHYSICAL BEAUTY AND AN ATTRACTIVE appearance were admired in ancient Greece in both men and women. Clothes were styled simply. Both sexes wore long tunics, draped loosely for comfort in the warm climate, and held in place with decorative pins or brooches. A heavy cloak was added for travelling or in bad weather. The tunics of soldiers and labourers were cut short, so they would not get in the way. Clothes were made of wool and linen, which were spun at home. Fabrics were coloured with dyes made from plants, insects and shellfish. The rich could afford more luxurious garments made from imported cotton or silk. Sandals were usually worn outdoors, though men sometimes wore boots. In hot weather hats made of straw or wool kept off the sun. A tan was not admired because it signified outdoor work as a labourer or a slave. Men wore their hair short, and women wore it long, coiled up in elaborate styles sometimes decorated with ribbons.

SEE FOR YOURSELF
Glass mirrors were not known to the Greeks. Instead, they used highly polished bronze to see their reflection in. This mirror has a handle in the shape of a woman. Winged sphinxes sit on her shoulders.

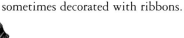

GOLDEN LION
This heavy bracelet dates from around the 4th or 5th century BC. It is made of solid gold and decorated with two lion heads. Gold was valuable because there was little of it to be found in Greece itself. Most of it was imported from Asia Minor or Egypt.

KEEP IT SIMPLE
The figurine above is wearing a peplos. This was a simple, sleeveless dress worn by Greek women. The only adornment was a belt tied underneath the bust. This statue comes from a Greek colony in southern Italy.

CHITON
You will need: tape measure, rectangle of cloth, scissors, pins, chalk, needle, thread, 12 metal buttons (with loops), cord.

1 Ask a friend to measure your width from wrist to wrist, double this figure. Measure your length from shoulder to ankle. Cut your cloth to these figures.

2 Fold the fabric in half widthways. Pin the two sides together. Draw a chalk line along the fabric, 2cm away from the edge of the fabric.

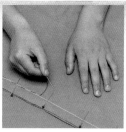

3 Sew along the chalk line. Then turn the material inside out, so the seam is on the inside. Refold the fabric so the seam is at the back.

TEXTILE TRADE

Clothes in ancient Greece were usually made from wool and linen. The Greeks exported their wool, which was admired for its superior quality. Cotton and silk were imported to make clothes. But only wealthy Greeks could afford clothes made from these materials.

cotton

raw wool

linen

POWDER POT

Greek women used face powder and other cosmetics and kept them in a ceramic pot called a pyxis. This one was was made in Athens in about 450BC. The painted decoration shows women spinning and weaving.

Clothes were hand-made in ancient Greece. Enough material would be woven to fit the person they were being made for exactly, to avoid waste.

spiral band

BURIAL JEWELLERY

Some pieces of jewellery, like the ones pictured here, were made especially for burial. Very thin sheet gold was beaten into belts and wreaths. Important people like the Kings and Queens of Macedonia were buried in crowns of gold leaves.

belt

wreath

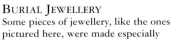

4 Make a gap big enough for your head to fit in, at one of the open ends of the fabric. Mark where the gap is going to be and pin the fabric together there.

5 From the head gap mark a point every 5cm to the end of the fabric. Pin together the front and back along these points. Your arms will fit through here.

6 At each pin, sew on a button to hold the two sides of material together. To secure the button, sew through the loop several times and knot it.

7 Cut a length of cord, to fit around your waist with a little bit spare to tie. Tie this cord around your waist and bunch the material up, over the cord.

Gods and Goddesses

The ancient Greeks believed that their gods looked like human beings and felt human emotions that led them to quarrel and fall in love. People also thought that the gods had magical powers and were immortal (meaning that they could live forever). With these powers, the gods could become invisible or disguise themselves and even turn people into animals. The gods were thought to influence all parts of human life and were kept busy with requests for help, from curing illness to ensuring a victory in war. In order to keep on the right side of the gods, individuals made sacrifices, left offerings and said prayers to them. Communities financed the building of temples, such as the Parthenon, paid for priests to look after them and organized festivals all in honour of the gods.

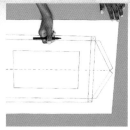

WINGED MESSENGER
Hermes was the god of eloquence and good luck. He was known for his mischievous and adventure-seeking nature. Zeus made him a messenger to the gods, to try and keep him occupied and out of trouble.

KING OF THE GODS
Zeus ruled over earth and heaven from Mount Olympus, (a real place on the border of Macedonia). He was thought to be a fair god who upheld order and justice. Wrongdoers could be punished with thunderbolts thrown by him.

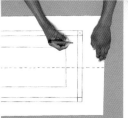

WILD GODDESS
Artemis was the goddess of wild places and animals, hunting and the moon. She was a skilful archer, whose arrows caused death and plagues. The power to heal was another of her attributes.

PARTHENON

You will need: two pieces of white card 62cm by 38.5cm, ruler, black felt-tip pen, shoebox, scissors, blue, red and cream paint, paintbrush, PVA glue, piece of red corrugated card (approximately 39cm x 28.5cm), masking tape, craft knife, 160cm of balsa wood.

1 Draw a horizontal line across the centre of the card. Place the shoebox in the middle. Draw around it. Draw a second box 7cm away from this.

2 Draw a third box 2cm away from the second. Extend the lines of the second box to meet the third, to form four tabs, one in each corner.

3 To make the ends of the roof, draw half a diamond shape along the edge of the second box. Add on two rectangular tabs 1cm deep.

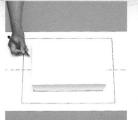

LOVE AND PROTECTION

Aphrodite was the goddess of love and beauty. Her vanity was instrumental in causing one of the biggest campaigns in Greek folklore, the Trojan War. Aphrodite promised to win Paris (son of the king of Troy) the love of the most beautiful mortal woman in the world – Helen. In return, Paris was to name Aphrodite as the most beautiful of all the goddesses. However, Helen was already married to the king of Sparta. When she left him to join Paris, the Greeks declared war on Troy. A bloodthirsty war followed in which heroes and gods clashed.

SYMBOLS

Each god and goddess was thought to be responsible for particular aspects of daily life. Each was represented by a symbol. Wheat symbolized Demeter, goddess of living things. Dionysus, god of the vine and wine, was appropriately represented by grapes.

wheat   *grapes*

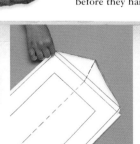

A POWERFUL FAMILY

Hera was the wife of Zeus and goddess of marriage. She was revered by women as the protector of their married lives. Her own marriage was marked by conflicts between herself and her husband. Her jealousy of rivals for her unfaithful husband's affections led her to persecute them. She was also jealous of Heracles, who was Zeus' son by another woman. Hera sent snakes to kill Heracles when he was a baby. Fortunately for Heracles, he had inherited his father's strength and killed the snakes before they harmed him.

GRAPES OF JOY

The god Dionysus was admired for his sense of fun. As god of fertility, the vine and wine, he was popular with both male and female worshippers. However, his followers were too enthusiastic for some city-states which banned celebrations in his name.

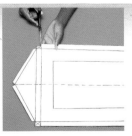

4 Repeat step 3 for the other end of the roof. Cut out both ends of the roof and cut into the four corner tabs. Get your painting equipment ready.

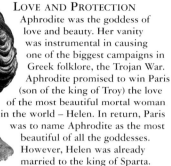

5 Turn the roof piece over. Draw and then paint the above design on to each end piece. Paint a blue, 1cm margin along each side. Leave to dry.

6 Turn the card over. Fold up all the sides of the second box. Fold in each corner tab and glue to its adjoining side. Fold down the rectangular tabs.

7 Cut the piece of red corrugated card in half. Stick them together with tape, along the unridged side. Turn them over and fold along the middle.

Temples and Festivals

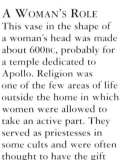

Festivals to honour the gods were important public occasions in ancient Greece. At the heart of each festival was a temple. At festival time, people flocked to the cities from the countryside. The greatest festivals were occasions of splendour and celebration. They involved processions, music, sports, prayers, animal sacrifices and offerings of food, all of which took place at the temple. The earliest Greek temples were built of wood, and none have survived. Later, temples built from stone echoed the simplicity of tree trunks in their columns and beams. The finest temples were made from marble. They were often decorated with brightly painted friezes, showing mythical stories of gods, goddesses and heroes. No expense was spared because temples were thought to be the gods' earthly homes. Each temple housed a statue of the god to which it was dedicated. The statues were usually elaborate and occasionally made from precious materials such as gold and ivory.

A Woman's Role
This vase in the shape of a woman's head was made about 600BC, probably for a temple dedicated to Apollo. Religion was one of the few areas of life outside the home in which women were allowed to take an active part. They served as priestesses in some cults and were often thought to have the gift of seeing into the future.

Grand Entrance
The monumental gateways to the temple complex on top of the Acropolis were called the Propylaea. The temple beside it honoured Athena who is shown as Nike, goddess of victory.

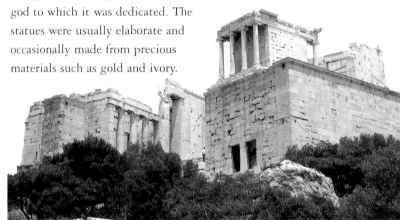

8 Glue the ends of the corrugated card to the folded up edges of the painted card. Leave to dry. This piece forms the roof to your temple.

9 Draw around the shoebox, on to the second piece of card. Draw another box 7cm away. Cut it out, leaving a 1cm border. This is the temple base.

10 Ask an adult to help you with this step. Cut out 32 columns from balsa wood. Each must be 5cm in height. Paint them cream and leave to dry.

11 Mark eight points along each edge of the second box by drawing around a column piece. Draw them an equal distance from each other.

A BIRTHDAY PARADE

A parade of horsemen, chariots and people leading sacrificial animals all formed part of the procession of the annual Panathenaic festival. It was held once a year, in Athens, to celebrate the goddess Athena's birthday. Every fourth year, the occasion involved an even more elaborate ceremony which lasted for six days. During the festivities, the statue of Athena was presented with a new robe.

A TEMPLE FOR THREE GODS

The Erectheum was built on the Acropolis, looking down on Athens 100 m below. Unusually for a Greek temple, it housed the worship of more than one god: the legendary king Erectheus; Athena, guardian goddess of the city of Athens, and Poseidon, god of the sea. The columns in the shape of women are called caryatids.

BUILDING MATERIALS

Big buildings were often put up near a quarry or navigable water. Limestone was the most commonly used stone, and pine and cypress the commonest woods. Costly marble and cedar were reserved for temples and palaces.

marble   limestone

pine

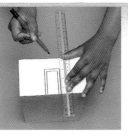

THE LION'S MOUTH

This gaping lion is actually a waterspout from an Athenian temple built in about 570BC. Although rainfall in Greece is low, waterspouts were necessary to allow storm water to drain off buildings with flat roofs. The lion was chosen as a symbol of strength and power.

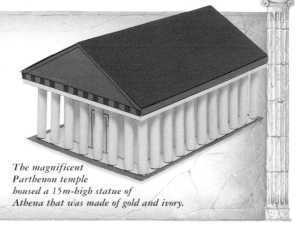

12 Draw a door on to a short end of the shoebox. Glue the roof on to the top of the shoebox. Paint the 1cm border on the temple base, blue.

13 Glue the columns into place, between the roof and the base. Dab glue on to their ends. Position them on the circles marked out in step 11.

The magnificent Parthenon temple housed a 15m-high statue of Athena that was made of gold and ivory.

Religion and Worship

THE ORACLE AT DELPHI
It was believed that the Oracle could read the future. Its home was in a cave at Delphi, where it spoke through a woman called the Pythia. She was an ordinary woman who took the job for life and never married. The Pythia is shown above, holding a laurel leaf and a libation bowl.

THE WORSHIP OF GODS and goddesses was at the heart of life in ancient Greece. Each god or goddess was in charge of a particular aspect of life, and the Greeks offered prayers and sacrifices according to their needs. The Greek people organized religious festivals, which were celebrated as major public holidays, and gave money to build temples and shrines. Pilgrims seeking favours or forgiveness from the gods made journeys which were often long and hard to sacred places.

The most sacred place of all was the shrine at Delphi in central Greece, which was dedicated to the god Apollo. The Greeks believed Delphi was the centre of the world. Individuals or families could worship privately at a shrine when they felt the need to do so, instead of gathering together with others on a special day. People offered prayers and sacrifices themselves, or they could ask a priest or priestess to approach the god on their behalf. Priests often came from a local noble family. Some inherited their position, others were elected or appointed by a city, others paid for the privilege of being a priest. Priests were highly respected, but their job was only a part-time one.

ASK HERE
Questions for the Oracle were submitted in writing to the priests at the Oracle's cave, shown here. Wealthy people made animal sacrifices and paid large sums of money to hear the Oracle's predictions on personal matters such as love or business. Cities sent for advice on matters of public interest and importance. To prepare herself to receive the Oracle's answers, the Pythia first inhaled vapours from the Castalian spring and went into a trance. Her words were then interpreted for the enquirer by the priests.

FAMILY OFFERINGS

On this relief, carved around 200BC, a family is gathered to honour a statue of Zeus. As head of the household, the father leads the ritual. Standing at the altar, he holds a dish that might contain wine, oil or honey. Major occasions involved the sacrifice of an animal. Lesser ones might require an offering of cakes or fruit, or just a pinch of incense.

ACT OF WORSHIP

This female figure was found at a holy sanctuary and is dated around 2000BC. It is thought to be a woman raising her arms in an act of worship. There were rules on how to address the different gods. To speak to most gods, a worshipper held their arms up to the sky. Underworld gods were addressed with the arms turned down. To communicate with marine gods the worshipper faced the sea water.

SACRIFICE TO THE GODS

This wooden panel, painted near Corinth around 500BC, shows a worshipper with musicians and priests about to sacrifice a sheep. Usually the meat was cooked and distributed amongst the worshippers, to be eaten. The fat and bones of the animal would be left on the altar for the gods. Animals were also sacrificed as a means of telling the future. Healthy organs meant good fortune, but diseased organs signified bad luck.

SPECIAL STOREHOUSE

This building was one of over a dozen treasuries built at Delphi to hold statues and precious offerings to the gods. The storehouses were ruined by an earthquake, and their contents plundered by treasure-hunters. Some storehouses, including this one, have been rebuilt by archaeologists.

Heroes and Myths

GREEK MYTHOLOGY IS RICH in stories of victorious heroes and heroines, quarrelling gods and goddesses and mysterious and unusual creatures. While keeping people entertained, the stories also tried to answer questions about how the world and humans came into existence. These powerful tales provided inspiration for ancient Greek art and material for their plays. In addition to this, they served as a valuable historical record and encouraged the Greeks to take pride in their vibrant cultural past. Traditionally, mythical stories were passed down through generations by word of mouth. Sometimes travelling bards were paid to recite poems which they had learnt by heart. Eventually, these tales came to be written down. The earliest of these that survive are thought to be the work of the poet Homer. Two poems that we know about are *The Odyssey* and *The Iliad*. Both tell tales of heroes battling against supernatural forces.

MONSTER KILLER

According to Greek legend the Minotaur was half-bull and half-man. It lived in a maze called the labyrinth on the island of Crete. Many people had entered the maze but never come out. Each year the people of Athens were forced to send human sacrifices to feed the bull. The hero Theseus made it his mission to kill the Minotaur. A princess presented Theseus with a sword and a ball of string to help him. Theseus unwound the string as he walked through the maze. After killing the Minotaur he followed the string back to the entrance of the cave.

SNAKE STRANGLER

The super-strong Heracles was the only human being to become a Greek god. This Roman fresco shows him as a baby strangling serpents sent by the jealous goddess Hera to kill him.

HEAD OF MEDUSA

You will need: board, self-drying modelling clay, rolling pin, ruler, modelling tool, pencil, sandpaper, acrylic paints, one small and one large paintbrush, varnish (1 part water to 1 part PVA glue).

1 With a rolling pin, roll out a slab of clay 20cm by 20cm and 2cm thick. With the modelling tool, cut out a head in the shape shown in the picture.

2 Shape a small piece of clay into a nose. Mould it on to the head with your fingers. Use the modelling tool to smooth the edges into the face.

3 Carve a mouth with lots of teeth and two eyes and etch a gruesome design into the head. Press the end of a pencil into the eyes to make eyeballs.

STONY STARE

Medusa was a winged monster with hair of snakes. She was one of three such female gorgons. Medusa had a face so horrific that any human who looked directly at it was turned to stone. The only way to kill her was to cut off her head. Medusa, whose name means "cunning", outwitted several would-be killers. The hero Perseus finally killed her with help from Athena and Hermes. They lent Perseus a magic cap to make him invisible, a sickle to cut off Medusa's head and a shield in which to see her reflection. Even dead, Medusa remained powerful. Perseus killed his enemy Polydectes by forcing him to look at her face.

FOOLING THE GIANT

King Odysseus was a mythical hero who had many adventures. One escapade found him captured in a cave by a one-eyed giant. To escape, Odysseus stabbed out the giant's eye and rode out of the cave clinging to the underside of a ram.

The word gorgon in Greek suggests the monster's glaring eyes.

FLYING HORSE

The winged horse Pegasus appeared on the coins of Corinth as the city's symbol. Pegasus helped Bellerophon, a Corinthian hero, in his battles. First against the Chimaera which was a monster with a lion's head, a goat's middle and a snake's tail and then against the Amazons, a race of female warriors.

4 Between the palms of your hands, roll out four thin strips of clay to represent the snakes on Medusa's head. Press them into place as shown above.

5 Press a finger down on the end of each roll to make a snake's head. Use the modelling tool and pencil to carve in scales on the snakes' bodies.

6 The head needs to dry completely before you can paint the face. To dry it, let it sit for a few hours on either side. Be careful when you turn it over.

7 When the head is completely dry, sand with fine sandpaper. Paint the face in black, red, white and gold as shown here. Leave to dry and varnish.

Death and the Underworld

PEOPLE IN ANCIENT GREECE would live only about half as long as people in the West do today. It was common for sickly children to die in infancy. Large numbers of men were killed in battle, women often died in childbirth and epidemics could wipe out whole communities.

Most Greeks believed that after death, their souls roamed the Underworld, a cold and gloomy region where the wicked were sent to be punished. In *The Odyssey* the hero Achilles says, "I'd rather be a common labourer on Earth working for a poor man than lord of all the legions of the dead." Very few people, it was thought were good enough to be sent to the Isles of the Blessed. If they were, they could spend eternity amusing themselves with sports and music. People who had led exceptional lives (such as the hero Heracles) were thought destined to become gods and live on Mount Olympus.

When someone died, their body was either buried or cremated. The Greeks believed that only when the body or ashes had been covered with earth, could its spirit leave for the Underworld. Graves contained possessions for use in the afterlife, and women left offerings of food and drink at the graveside to help the spirits.

FRAGRANT FAREWELL
Graves were sometimes marked with lekythoi, white clay flasks holding a perfumed oil that had been used to anoint the body. The lekythoi were usually painted with farewell scenes, funerals or images of the dead.

FOOD FOR THOUGHT
The tradition of leaving food at gravesides began in Mycenaean times. Then people could be buried with their armour, cooking pots and even pets and slaves to accompany them. By 300BC the Greeks were leaving food such as wine and eggs at gravesides as nourishment for the dead.

wine

eggs

A DIVE INTO THE UNKNOWN
The figure on the painting above is shown leaping from life into the ocean of death. The pillars were put up by Heracles to mark the end of the known, living world. This diver was found painted on the walls of a tomb.

TUG OF LOVE

This painting from a vase shows Persephone with Hades, her husband and ruler of the underworld. Hades dragged Persephone from earth down to the Underworld. Her distraught mother, the goddess Demeter, neglected the crops to search for her. Zeus intervened and decided that Persephone would spend six months of every year with her mother and the other six with Hades. Whenever her daughter returned in spring, Demeter would look after the crops. However, Demeter grew sad each time her daughter went back to the Underworld and wintertime would set in.

LAST JOURNEY

The body of a dead person was taken from their home to the grave by mourners bearing tributes. To express their grief, they might cut off their hair, tear at their cheeks with their nails until blood flowed, and wear black robes. If there was a funeral feast at the graveside, the dishes were smashed afterwards and left there.

ROYAL TOMB

Women were less likely to be honoured by tombstone portraits than men. Philis, seen above, was an exception to this rule, possibly because she was the daughter of a powerful Spartan king. Athens enforced a law against extravagant tombs. No more than 10 men could be employed for any more than three days to build one.

A Trip to the Theatre

THE FIRST GREEK DRAMAS were performed at temples in honour of the gods. The stories they told were a mixture of history and myth, and featured the adventures of famous Greeks as well as the exploits of gods and legendary heroes. The all-male cast was backed up by a chorus of singers and dancers, who provided a commentary on the action. Drama became so popular that large open-air theatres were built in major cities and at sacred places such as Delphi and Epidauros. Prizes were awarded to the best dramatists. The three most famous writers of tragedies were Aeschylus, Sophocles and Euripides. They wrote over 300 plays between them, but only a tenth survive. The works of another 150 known writers have all been lost. Greek drama is still performed in theatres today.

SEAT OF HONOUR
Most theatre-goers sat on stone benches. This carved chair might have been reserved for an important official or a sponsor who had paid the expenses of a public performance.

THEATRE
Large theatres like this one at Ephesus on the coast of modern Turkey had excellent acoustics and could hold an audience of over 10,000. The stage, a circle of beaten earth in the centre of the theatre, was called the orchestra, which means dancing floor.

BIRD MASK
You will need: balloon, petroleum jelly, papier-mâché (newspaper soaked in 1 part water to 2 parts PVA glue), black pen, scissors, paint, paintbrush, 2 pieces of ochre card (20cm x 10cm), glue stick, pair of compasses, two pieces of red card (40cm x 40cm), cord.

1 Blow up a balloon to head-size. Cover front and sides in petroleum jelly. Add several layers of papier-mâché. When this is dry, pop the balloon.

2 Ask a friend to mark the position of your eyes and the top of your ears on the mask. Cut out small holes at these points. Paint the mask as shown at the end.

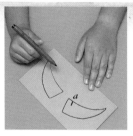

3 Draw and cut out two beak shapes. Repeat for both pieces of ochre card. Mark a point 1cm along the bottom of the beak (the edge marked *a* above).

44

COMIC TURN

A figurine from the 2nd century BC shows a masked comic actor sitting on an altar. He is hiding in a temple to escape punishment. Comedies were much enjoyed, but considered inferior to tragedies.

PLAYING PARTS

Greek actors wore masks to represent different characters and emotions. The same actor could play different roles in one drama by changing his mask. All the players were male, but some took female roles. Women were not allowed on the stage, and may even have been barred from joining the audience.

SUFFERING COMEDY

In this comic scene the actor in the middle plays the part of a centaur called Cheiron. Centaurs were mythical creatures that were half-man and half-horse. Cheiron was the wisest of them all. But he was also seen as a figure of fun because he was immortal yet suffered from a fatal wound.

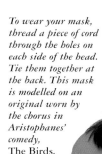

To wear your mask, thread a piece of cord through the holes on each side of the head. Tie them together at the back. This mask is modelled on an original worn by the chorus in Aristophanes' comedy, The Birds.

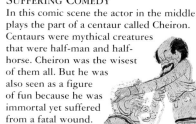

4 Draw a line from the corner of the top edge (*b*) to this point. Fold back the line. Glue the two pieces together along the top edge. Repeat.

5 Put the compass point in the corner of the red card. Draw two arcs, one with a 10cm radius and one with a 20cm radius. Cut out as one piece.

6 Cut feather shapes into the top of the red card. Draw an arc 5cm from the bottom. Cut out 14 tabs, as shown. Repeat both steps for the other piece of card.

7 Glue the two red cards together at the top. Glue the tabs down on to the top of the mask. Glue the beak pieces to the mask. Draw on the eyes.

45

Music and Dance

MUSIC AND DANCE WERE BOTH AN important part of Greek life. People sang, played and danced at religious ceremonies. Music was enjoyed for pleasure and entertainment at family celebrations, dramatic performances, feasts and drinking parties. Few written records remain of the notes played, but examples of the instruments do. The most popular instruments were the pipes. They were wind instruments similar to the oboe or clarinet. One pipe on its own was called the *aulos*, two played together were known as *auloi*. The stringed lyre and flute were other popular instruments. The stringed lyre produced solemn and dignified music. It was often played by men of noble birth to accompany a poetry recital. The flute was more usually played by slaves or dancing girls.

BREATH CONTROL
The leather strap tied around the auloi-player's cheeks helped to focus the power of his breath. One tube of the auloi supplied the melody, while the other produced an accompanying drone to give more depth to the sound. The aulos had as few as three or as many as 24 fingerholes for making the different notes.

Greek soldiers complained that lack of music was a hardship of war. Spartan soldiers resolved this problem by blowing tunes on pipes as they marched. Music was believed to have magical powers. Greek legend tells of Orpheus soothing savage beasts by playing his lyre. Another myth tells how Amphion (a son of Zeus) made stones move on their own and built a wall around the city of Thebes, by playing his lyre.

BANG! CRASH!
The bronze figurine above is playing the cymbals. They made a sound similar to castanets. The Greeks used the cymbals to accompany dancing. Other percussion instruments included wooden clappers and hand-held drums, like tambourines.

TIMPANON

You will need: scissors, corrugated card, tape measure, plate, white card, pair of compasses, pencil, PVA glue, tape, strips of newspaper, cream paper, red and purple felt-tip pens, ochre card, red and yellow ribbons.

1 Cut out a strip of corrugated card 5cm wide. Wrap it around a dinner plate. Add 6cm on to the length of this card and cut it off.

2 Put the plate upside down on the white card. Draw around it. Draw another circle 3cm inside the first. Cut this out to make a ring.

3 Glue the cardboard strip that you made in step 1 to the edge of the cardboard ring you made in step 2. Then tape them together for extra hold.

DIVINE MUSIC

Terpsichore was one of the Nine Muses, or spirits of the arts. She was the spirit of dance and music. Here Terpsichore plays a harp while her attendants hold the lyre and auloi. Other Muses included Polyhymnia, the spirit of hymns, and Euterpe, the spirit of flute-playing.

PERCUSSION

The timpanon was a tambourine made of animal skin, stretched over a frame. It was tapped to provide rhythmic accompaniment at dances or recitals. Stringed and wind instruments were thought superior because they made fitting music for solemn or exclusive occasions. Drums, cymbals and clappers were associated with buskers.

To play the timpanon tap on it with your fingers, as the ancient Greeks would have done.

ENTERTAINING

In this plate painting a young man plays the auloi while his female companion dances. Professional musicians were often hired to entertain guests at dinner parties. Sometimes the musicians were household slaves.

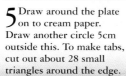

4 Make up some papier mâché solution with 1 part glue to 2 parts water. Soak strips of newspaper in it and cover the card ring with the wet strips.

5 Draw around the plate on to cream paper. Draw another circle 5cm outside this. To make tabs, cut out about 28 small triangles around the edge.

6 Draw the design shown above on to the paper. Place the paper over the top of the card ring. Dab glue on each tab and stick on to the corrugated card.

7 Cut a strip of ochre card big enough to fit around the timpanon. Decorate it as above and glue on. Make 4 bows with the ribbons and glue around the edge.

Arts and Crafts

THE ARTISTS AND CRAFTWORKERS of ancient Greece were admired for the quality of their work. They produced many objects of art including beautiful pottery, fine jewellery and impressive sculptures. Materials they worked with included stone, gold, silver, glass, gemstones and bronze. They also used wood, leather, bone, ivory and horn. Most goods were made on a small scale in workshops surrounding the market-place (*agora*). A craftsman might work on his own or with the help of his family and a slave or two. In the larger workshops of such cities as Athens, slaves laboured to produce bulk orders of popular goods. These might include shields, pottery and metalwork which were traded around the Mediterranean Sea for a large profit.

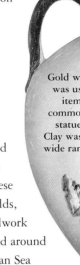

BULK PRODUCTION
Above is a terracotta mould, and on the right, the casting taken from it. Making a mould was a skilled and time-consuming task. Using a mould made it possible to produce items faster and more cheaply than carving each piece individually.

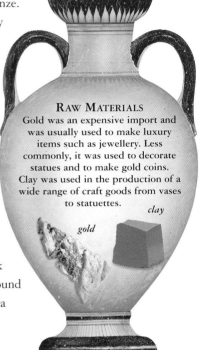

RAW MATERIALS
Gold was an expensive import and was usually used to make luxury items such as jewellery. Less commonly, it was used to decorate statues and to make gold coins. Clay was used in the production of a wide range of craft goods from vases to statuettes.

clay

gold

PANATHENAIC VASE
You will need: balloon, bowl, PVA glue, water, newspaper, two rolls of masking tape, black pen, scissors, sheet of paper 42cm x 30cm, card, pencil, paintbrush, black and cream paint.

1 Blow up the balloon. Cover it with two layers of papier mâché (paper soaked in one part glue, two parts water). Leave on one side to dry.

2 Using a roll of masking tape as a guide, draw and cut out two holes at the top and bottom of the balloon. Throw away the burst balloon.

3 Roll the sheet of paper into a tube. Make sure that it will fit through the middle of the roll of masking tape. Secure the tube with tape or glue.

VASE PAINTING

Black-figure vase painting originated in Corinth around 700BC. The black-figure style was succeeded by a red-figure style invented in Athens around 525BC. The painters were not all anonymous artisans. Many were widely recognized as artists in their own right who signed their works. The export of vases like this became a major source of income for both cities.

HOT WORK

In this scene two blacksmiths are forging metal at a brick furnace. Metal goods were expensive to produce. The furnaces themselves were fuelled by charcoal (burnt wood) which was expensive to make because wood was scarce in Greece. In addition, supplies of metal often had to be imported, sometimes from great distances. For example, tin, which was mixed with local copper to make bronze, was brought from southern Spain.

Amphorae like this one were given as prizes at the Panathenaic games. They were decorated with sporting images.

GOLD PECTORAL

This gold pectoral, made on the island of Rhodes in the 7th century BC, was meant to be worn across the breast. Gold was rare in Greece. It was usually imported at great expense from surrounding areas such as Egypt or Asia Minor.

4 Push the tube through the middle of the balloon. Tape into place. Push a roll of masking tape over the bottom of the paper tube and tape.

5 Tape the second roll of masking tape to the top of the tube. Make sure that both rolls are securely attached at either end of the paper tube.

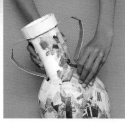

6 Cut two strips of card, 15cm long. Attach them to either side of the vase, as seen above. Cover the entire vase with papier mâché, and leave to dry.

7 Using a pencil, copy the pattern seen on the vase in the picture above on to your vase. Carefully paint in the pattern and leave on one side to dry.

Sports and Fitness

Fitness was valued as an essential preparation for war. But the Greeks also enjoyed sport for its own sake, and most cities had a public gymnasium, where men gathered to train and to relax. They preferred individual contests to team games, and often celebrated religious festivals by running races to honour the gods. This is how the Olympic Games first began in 776BC. It was held every four years, and expanded to include long jump, throwing the discus and javelin, boxing, wrestling, chariot races and horse races, as well as poetry and drama competitions. There was also a gruesome fighting sport called *pankration* (total power), a combination of boxing and wrestling in which the only forbidden tactics were eye-gouging and biting. During the Olympics, all wars between cities stopped, so that people could journey safely to the Games. Women were banned from competing or watching the Olympics but they had their own games, also held at Olympia in honour of the goddess Hera.

THE WINNER
A Greek king (on the right) hands a wreath of victory to an Olympic winner. A priest stands by to remind contestants that they are on sacred ground. There were no cash prizes at the Olympics. However, because they brought honour to their cities, winners were sometimes given money on their return home, or even free meals for life.

SPORTING STARS
This vase painting shows a long-jumper holding weights, a discus thrower and two men with javelins. They represent three of the five sports that made up the *pentathlon* (*penta* is Greek for five). The other two were running and wrestling. The pentathlon began with a foot race, which was followed by javelin throwing, then discus throwing and finished with the long jump. The two contestants who scored highest in these events then wrestled one another to decide the overall winner. Most sportsmen were amateurs. There were also many professionals who trained and competed for a single event.

SPORTING FACILITIES

Much of ancient Olympia, where the first Olympic Games were held, has been uncovered by archaeologists working there since 1829. There were many facilities serving the competitors and spectators. At the centre of the complex were two large temples dedicated to Hera and Zeus. Amongst the buildings surrounding the temples were a hostel, restaurants, a huge gymnasium for training in and a hippodrome for horse and chariot races. Despite its size, Olympia never became a city, because it had no permanent citizens or local government.

DANGEROUS GAME

At the end of a chariot race, an armed man jumped off of the moving vehicle and ran a foot race. This event was eventually dropped from the Games because it often provoked laughter at undignified accidents instead of admiration for the competitors' skill. Chariots frequently overturned with disastrous results. As many as 40 competitors might take part, racing 12 laps of a 1,100 m circuit. The winner was the owner of the chariot and horses, not the driver.

GOING THE DISTANCE

Long-jumpers carried heavy weights to give them more momentum. The weights also helped them to balance. They jumped on to a bed of crumbled earth (skamma) raked smooth. This helped them to avoid injuries and leave a clear footprint so that the judges could measure the distance they had covered.

GETTING READY

An athlete binds his hair with a cloth to keep it out of the way. Most athletes competed naked in the Olympic Games. It was felt that sport glorified male strength and beauty. When women competed against each other in the games to honour Hera, they wore short tunics.

STEP THIS WAY

Competitors taking part in the original Olympic Games entered the stadium through this archway. The grassy embankments surrounding the stadium could seat up to 40,000 spectators.

Science and Philosophy

T HE GREEKS COULD AFFORD to devote time to studying and thinking because their civilization was both wealthy and secure. They learned astrology from the Babylonians, and mathematics from the Egyptians. They used their scientific knowledge to develop many practical inventions, including water clocks, cogwheels, gearing systems, slot machines and steam engines. However, these devices were not widely used as there were many slave workers to do the jobs.

The word "philosophy"comes from the Greek word *philosophos*, meaning love of knowledge. The Greeks developed many different branches of philosophy. Three of these were politics (how best to govern), ethics (how to behave well) and cosmology (how the universe worked). Greek philosophers recognized the value of experimenting. But they could not always see their limitations. Aristotle discovered that evaporation turned salt water into fresh water, and wrongly assumed wine would turn into water by the same process.

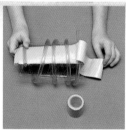

CLOCK TOWER
The Tower of the Winds in Athens contains a water clock. The original Egyptian invention was a bucket of water with a tiny hole in the bottom. As the water dripped out of it, the water level fell past scored marks on the inside of the bucket, measuring time. The Greeks improved on this design, using the flow of water to work a dial with a moving pointer.

GREAT THINKER
The philosopher Aristotle (384–322BC) is often recognized as the founder of Western science. He pioneered a rational approach to the world, based on observing and recording evidence. For three years, he was the tutor of Alexander the Great.

ARCHIMEDES SCREW
You will need: clean, empty plastic bottle, scissors, modelling clay, strong tape, length of clear plastic tube, bowl of water, blue food colouring, empty bowl.

1 Cut off the bottle top. Place the modelling clay into the middle of the bottle, about 5cm from the end. Punch a hole here with the scissors.

2 Cut a strip of tape the same length as the bottle. Tape it to the middle of the bottle. This will give the tube extra grip later on.

3 Twist the length of tube around the bottle. Go from one end of the bottle to the other. Tape the tube into place over the first piece of tape.

WATER LIFTER

When the Archimedes screw is turned, it lifts water from one level to another. It is named after its inventor, the scientist Archimedes, who lived about 287–211BC, in Syracuse, Sicily. It is still in use today.

FATHER OF GEOMETRY

Euclid (about 330–260BC) was a mathematician. He lived in the Greek-Egyptian city of Alexandria. He is known as the father of geometry, which comes from the Greek word for "measuring land". Geometry is the study of points, lines, curves, surfaces and their measurements. His geometry textbook was called *Elements*. It was still widely used in the early part of the 20th century AD, over 2,000 years after his death. This picture shows the front page of an edition of the book that was printed in London in 1732.

4 Place a few drops of the blue food colouring into the bowl of water. Stir it in so that the colour mixes evenly throughout the water.

5 Place one end of the bottle into the bowl of blue water. Make sure that the tube at the opposite end is pointing towards the empty bowl.

6 Twist the bottle around in the blue water. As you do so, you will see the water start travelling up the tube and gradually filling the other bowl.

The invention of the Archimedes screw made it possible for farmers to water their fields with irrigation channels. It saved them from walking back and forth to the river with buckets.

Medical Matters

THE GREEKS BELIEVED THAT ultimately only the gods had the power to heal wounds and cure sickness. But they also developed a scientific approach to medicine. Greek doctors could treat injuries and battle wounds by bandaging and bone-setting. They relied on rest, diet and herbal drugs to cure disease. However, they were powerless against large-scale epidemics, such as the plague. Doctors believed that good health was dependent on the balance between four main body fluids – blood, phlegm and yellow and black bile. If this balance was disturbed, they attempted to restore it by applying heated metal cups to the body to draw off harmful fluids. The sweat this produced convinced them it worked. This mistaken practice continued in Europe until the 17th century.

FATHER OF MEDICINE
Hippocrates founded a medical school around 400BC. He taught that observation of symptoms was more important than theory. His students took an oath to use their skills to heal and never to harm.

BODY BALANCE
Bleeding was a common procedure, intended to restore the body's internal balance. This carving shows surgical instruments and cups used for catching blood. Sometimes bleeding may have helped to drain off poisons, but more often it can only have weakened the patient.

HEALING GOD
The Greeks worshipped Asclepius, as the god of healing. He is shown here with a serpent, representing wisdom. Invalids seeking a cure made a visit to his shrine.

LEG OFFERING
You will need: self-drying modelling clay, rolling pin, board, ruler, modelling tool, paintbrush, cream acrylic paint.

1 Divide the clay into two pieces. With the rolling pin, roll out one piece to 15cm length, 10cm width and 2cm depth. This is the base for the leg.

2 Roll out the second piece of clay. With the modelling tool, carve out a leg and foot shape. It should be big enough to fit on one side of the base.

3 Gently place the leg on the right-hand side of the base. With the tool, draw a shallow outline around the leg into the base. Remove the leg.

THEORY AND PRACTICE

Patients would explain their dreams to doctors, who then prescribed treatment. In this relief, a healing spirit in the shape of a serpent visits a sleeping patient. In the foreground, the physician bandages the wounded arm.

NATURAL HEALING

The Greeks used a large variety of natural treatments to cure illnesses. Herbal remedies were particularly popular. Lentils, mustard and honey may have been combined in a poultice and applied to a wound.

lentils

mustard

honey

TOOL KIT

The Greeks used bronze surgical instruments, including forceps and probes. Surgery was usually a last resort. Even when it was successful, patients often died from the shock and pain, or from infection afterwards. Operations on limbs were more successful than those on body cavities such as the chest or stomach.

4 With the tool, score the outline with lines. Carve the ancient Greek message seen in the picture above next to the leg.

5 Mould the leg onto the scored area of the base. Use your fingers to press the sides of the leg in place. Carve toes and toenails into the foot.

6 Paint over the entire leg offering with a cream colour, to give it an aged look. Leave to dry overnight. Your leg offering is done.

This model is based on a real one left as a thank-offering to the god Asclepius by someone whose leg was affected by illness. This was a common practice in ancient Greece.

55

Travel and Trade

T HE MOUNTAINOUS LANDSCAPE of ancient Greece was too rocky for carts or chariots, so most people rode donkeys or walked. Sea travel was simpler – the many islands of the eastern Mediterranean made it possible to sail from one port to another without losing sight of land. Merchant ships were sailed because they were too heavy to be rowed. Greek sailors had no compasses. By day they relied on coastal landmarks and at night they navigated by the stars. However, neither method was reliable. A sudden storm could throw a ship off course or cause it to sink.

Merchant ships carried olive oil, wool, wine, silver, fine pottery and slaves. These goods were traded in return for wheat and timber, both of which were scarce in Greece. Other imported products included tin, copper, ivory, gold, silk and cotton.

COINAGE
The gold coin above shows Zeus, ruler of the gods, throwing a thunderbolt. Coins were invented in Lydia (in present-day Turkey) around 635BC, and introduced to Greece soon afterwards. Before that, the Greeks had used bars of silver and rods of iron as money. Greek coins were also made of silver, bronze and electrum, a mixture of gold and silver.

SEA GOD
Poseidon was the god of the sea, horses and earthquakes. Sailors prayed and made sacrifices to him, hoping for protection against storms, fogs and pirates. He is usually pictured holding a trident, the three-pronged spear used by Greek fishermen. At the trading port of Corinth, the Isthmian Games were held every other year in honour of Poseidon.

HARD CURRENCY
The first coins may have been used to pay mercenary soldiers, rather than for trading or collecting taxes. The earliest coins usually bore a religious symbol or the emblem of a city. Only later did they show the head of a ruler. The coin on the right shows the sea god Poseidon with his trident. The coin on the left bears the rose of Rhodes. Many countries that traded with the Greeks copied their idea of using coins for money.

SHIPPING

The ship on the right is a sail-powered merchantman. The criss-cross lines represent a wooden and rope catwalk stretched over the cargo, which was stored in an uncovered hold. Liquids such as wine and olive oil were transported and sold in long narrow pottery jars called amphorae, which could be neatly stacked in the hold. Merchant ships faced many dangers that could cause the loss of their cargo. Pirates and storms were the worst of these.

WEIGHING OUT

Most dry goods were sold loose and had to be weighed out on a balance such as this one. Officials would oversee the proceedings to ensure that they were fair. They stopped merchants and traders from cheating one another. In Athens, these officials were known as *metronomoi*. It was essential for merchants to familiarize themselves with the various systems of weights and measures used in different countries.

MARKET STALLS

The agora or market-place was to be found in the centre of every Greek town. Market stalls sold a wide range of goods including meat, vegetables, eggs, cheese and fish. Fish was laid out on marble slabs to keep it cool and fresh.

clams
prawns
mussels

RIDING

Mountainous countryside made travelling overland difficult in Greece. The few roads that did exist were in poor condition. For most people, walking was the only way to reach a destination. Horses were usually only used by wealthy people to travel on. Donkeys and mules were used by tradesmen to transport large loads. Longer journeys were made by boat.

Fighting Forces

ALL GREEK MEN were expected to fight in their city's army. In Sparta the army was on duty all year round. In other parts of Greece men gave up fighting in autumn to bring in the harvest and make the wine. The only full-time soldiers in these states were the personal bodyguards of a ruler or mercenaries who fought for anyone who paid them. Armies consisted mainly of hoplites (armoured infantry), cavalry (soldiers on horseback) and a group of foot soldiers armed with stones and bows and arrows. The hoplites were the most important fighting force as they engaged in hand-to-hand combat. The cavalry was less effective in war because riders had no stirrups, which made charging with a lance impossible, as the rider would fall off on contact. They were used for scouting, harassing a beaten enemy and carrying messages.

HARD HELMET
This bronze helmet from Corinth was fashioned to protect the face. It has guards for the cheeks and the bridge of the nose. Iron later replaced bronze as the main metal for weapons.

BOWMEN
The Greek army usually employed Scythian archers to fight for them. Archers were useful for fighting in mountainous countryside where they could position themselves above the enemy. Some Greeks soldiers did fight with bows and arrows. They fought in small units known as *psiloi*. But most of the soldiers in these units could only afford simple missile weapons, such as a javelin or slings from which they shot stones.

WARRIOR GREAVES
You will need: clear film, bowl of water, plaster bandages, sheet of paper, kitchen paper, scissors, cord, gold paint, paintbrush.

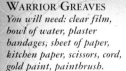

1 Ask a friend to help you with steps 1 to 3. Loosely cover both of your lower legs (from your ankle to the top of your knee) in clear film.

2 Soak each plaster bandage in water. Working from one side of your leg to the other, smooth the bandage over the front of each leg.

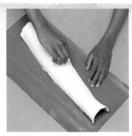

3 Carefully remove each greave. Set them on some paper. Dampen some kitchen paper and use it to smooth the greaves down. Leave them to dry.

A RARE SIGHT IN BATTLE

Chariots were not often used in warfare because they could only be used on flat plains. There were usually two people in the chariot, one to drive it, and the other to fight from the back of it.

FIGHTING FORCES

Tin and copper were used to make bronze, the main material for weapons and armour. Bronze is harder than pure copper and, unlike iron, does not rust. As there was no tin in Greece, it was imported from faraway lands.

copper   *tin*

HOPLITES

This fighting force was made up of middle-class men who could afford the weaponry. A hoplite's armoury consisted of a shield, helmet, spear, sword and greaves. Helmets were made of bronze and were usually crested with horsehair. The body was protected by a bronze cuirass, a one-piece breast- and back-plate, under which the hoplites wore a leather cuirass. Shields were usually round and decorated with a symbol.

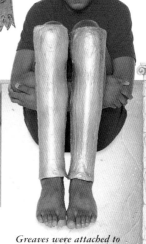

4 Trim the edges of the greaves, to make them look neat. Measure four lengths of cord to fit around your leg, below the knee and above the ankle.

5 Turn the greaves on to their front. Lay the cord in place at the point where you want to tie them to your leg. Fix them into place using wet bandages.

6 Leave the plaster bandages to dry, with the cord in place. Now paint each greave with gold paint. Once they are dry, tie them on.

Greaves were attached to the lower leg to protect it in battle. They were worn by hoplites.

Warfare

WHEN THE GREEKS WENT TO WAR it was usually to engage in raids and sieges of rival city states. Major battles with foreign powers were rare, but the results could be devastating. Army commanders had to choose their ground with care and rely on the discipline and training of their troops to carry through their overall plan. Once the fighting had started, it was almost impossible to control large masses of men or to change their orders. The death or flight of a few key leaders could cause a whole army to break up in chaos.

The core of a Greek army consisted of heavily armed foot soldiers (hoplites) who fought together in solid blocks called phalanxes. As long as they stayed calm, the soldiers were protected by their bristling spears, overlapping shields and sheer weight of numbers. If they panicked and broke up, it was easy for the enemy to pick off individual hoplites, weighed down by 30 kg of armour.

HEROES AT PLAY
Achilles and Ajax were legendary Greek heroes of the Trojan war. This vase shows them playing dice. This game was played by soldiers to while away the time or to decide the share-out of loot. The outcome of the game was sometimes interpreted as a symbol of fate and death.

GREEK TRICK
The Greeks ended the siege of Troy by leaving a wooden horse outside the city and pretending to sail away. The Trojans dragged the horse inside, not realizing that it was filled with Greek soldiers. The soldiers crept out of the horse at night and opened the city gates to let their comrades in. Together they overran the city.

CLOSE COMBAT
The Greek soldiers and heroes of Homer's time fought each other in a series of one-to-one duels. In this engraving, Greek and Trojan warriors are fighting hand to hand. However, as armies began to use more hoplites, methods of fighting changed to accommodate them. This involved men fighting together in a phalanx.

VICTORY AGAINST THE ODDS

At the battle of Issus in 333BC Alexander the Great (left) led the charge against the Persian king Darius (in the chariot). Darius fled in panic, and his much larger army broke up. The Persian army was made up of many different peoples from all over his vast empire. They spoke different languages and did not trust each other, making control harder. In contrast, Alexander had tight control and long experience of fighting with his troops.

SEA FIGHT

In 480BC, the battle of Salamis ended a Persian invasion into Greek territory. The Persians had more and faster ships, but the Greeks defeated them by luring them into narrow waters where these advantages were lost. Then the crowded Persian vessels were rammed to pieces by the much heavier Greek ships.

END OF AN EMPIRE

Greece won another decisive victory against Persia in 331BC. At the battle of Gaugemala the Persian cavalry outnumbered Alexander's almost five to one and the infantry two to one. Discipline, daring and determination overcame the odds and the Persian army lost the battle. Consequently, the Persian empire finally yielded to Alexander.

Glossary

A

Acropolis A sacred hill overlooking Athens on which temples were built.

agora A market place.

alphabet Letters used in writing. The first two letters of the Greek alphabet are alpha and beta, which give us our word alphabet.

amphora A jar with two handles used to store wine or olive oil.

andron The room in a Greek house where men entertained.

Archimedes screw A device for lifting water from one level to another, named after its inventor, the Greek scientist Archimedes.

aristocracy A system of government by wealthy and privileged people.

auloi A pair of musical pipes. One tube supplied the melody, while the other produced a background drone.

B

bleeding A process used by doctors. It was thought to drain off poisons, but often it can only have weakened the patient.

bronze A metal made by mixing tin with copper. Bronze was used for making armour.

C

Castalian spring A spring at Delphi that gave off vapours. The priestess inhaled them and went into a trance.

cavalry Soldiers on horseback. They were used mainly for scouting ahead and delivering messages.

centaur A mythical beast, half man, half horse.

city state A centre of government. Ancient Greece was made up of about 300 city states.

colony A settlement of people outside their own country. The Greeks founded many colonies around the Mediterranean Sea.

cosmology The study of the workings of the universe.

cuirass A one-piece breast and back plate worn by soldiers.

D

Delphi The place the Greeks believed to be the centre of the world, and the home of the Oracle.

democracy A system of government by the many. Every citizen has the right to vote and hold public office.

E

electrum A mixture of gold and silver, used for making coins.

ethics A branch of philosophy that considers good conduct and the rules that govern it.

F

flax A plant that yields fibres which are woven into a fabric called linen.

fresco A painting applied to damp plaster and used to decorate walls in the homes of wealthy Greeks.

G

geometry A branch of mathematics concerning measurements of lines, angles and surfaces. It was pioneered by the Greek scientist Euclid. In Greek, it means measuring the land.

gorgon A female monster of such horrific appearance that anyone who looked at her died.

greaves Armour for the legs.

H

helot A slave in Sparta.

K

knucklebones A favourite game of the Greeks. It involved flipping small animal bones from one side of the hand to the other without dropping them.

L

lekythoi White clay flasks used at funerals. They held fragrant oil for anointing the body and were painted with farewell scenes .

Linear A A script used by the Minoans. It remains undeciphered.

M

metic A foreigner resident in Athens. Metics had to pay extra taxes and serve in the military. They were not allowed to own land or marry an Athenian.

metronomoi Athenian officials whose job it was to stop merchants and traders from cheating one another. They oversaw the weighing out of dry goods.

Minoan The first great Greek civilization, and the first in Europe. It flourished on the island of Crete around 2000BC.

Minotaur A mythical beast, half man, half bull, that lived in a maze under a palace in Crete. It was slain by the hero Theseus.

monarchy Government by a king or queen.

mosaic A floor made of coloured pebbles set in patterns, and found in the houses of wealthy Greeks.

Mount Olympus Home of the

Greek gods and goddesses.

muse There were nine muses, or spirits of the arts, including Terpsichore, the spirit of dance and music.

Mycenaean The second great Greek civilization. The Mycenaeans dominated the Greek mainland from around 1600BC.

mythology Traditional stories about the exploits of gods and legendary heroes.

O

oligarchy Government by a group of rich and powerful people.

olive The fruit of the olive tree. An important crop in ancient Greece, olives were eaten as an appetizer or pressed to make olive oil. They were also used in medicine.

Olympic Games A sporting competition held every four years at Olympia in honour of the god Zeus. The first Games was held in 776BC.

omphalos An egg-shaped stone found at the holy sanctuary at Delphi. Omphalos means navel and this stone was thought to be the centre of the world.

Oracle A spirit that could see into the future. The Oracle was believed to live in a cave at Delphi. People paid large sums of money to hear the Oracle's predictions on personal and business matters.

ostracism Every year Athenians could banish an unpopular person from the city for ten years. Voters scratched the name of their choice on a piece of pottery called an ostrakon, so the procedure was called ostracism.

P

Panathenaic festival A yearly procession with sacrifices in honour of Athena, which took place at the Parthenon in Athens.

pankration A gruesome fighting sport that combines boxing and wrestling. (The name pankration means total power.)

Parthenon A temple on the Acropolis in Athens dedicated to the city's goddess, Athena.

pectoral Jewellery or armour worn on the breast or chest.

pentathlon Five sports – discus, javelin, running, wrestling and long jump with weights – that formed part of the Olympic Games. (Penta is Greek for five.)

peplos A robe presented to the goddess Athena once every four years at the Panathenaic festival.

phalanx A solid block of hoplites (foot soldiers) in battle.

philosophy A Greek word meaning love of knowledge. Philosophy is the discipline of thinking about the meaning of life.

polis A Greek city state.

politics The art and science of government (from polis, city state).

priest Someone who offered prayers and sacrifices on behalf of worshippers at a temple. This was a part-time job, and priests lived among the ordinary people. Some priests inherited their job, others were elected to it. Others still paid for the privilege of being a priest.

Propylaea The momumental gateways to the temple complex on top of the Acropolis.

pyxis A box used for storing face powder or other cosmetics.

Pythia The priestess who officiated at Delphi. She inhaled vapours from the Castalian spring to put her into a trance so that the Oracle could speak through her.

S

slaves People who were not free, but owned by their masters. Some were worked to death, others were treated well and given good jobs.

T

terracotta A composition of baked clay and sand used to make statues, figurines and pottery.

timpanon A tambourine made with animal skin.

tragedy A play that ends in disaster. It usually concerns a good and noble person with a fatal flaw in his character that ultimately causes his downfall.

tunic A loose robe worn as everyday clothing by Greek men and women. It was usually fastened at the shoulder with a brooch or pin.

U

underworld A mysterious place to which the spirits of the dead were believed to travel after burial.

W

water clock A bucket full of water with a hole in the bottom. The flow of water worked a dial, which told the time.

wet nurse A woman employed to breastfeed babies.

Index